Clasp

And the years pass until one generation dies
and their knowledge with them

(Lee Harwood, 'One, Two, Three')

CLASP

late-modernist poetry in London in the 1970s

edited by
Robert Hampson
and
Ken Edwards

Shearsman Books

Published in the United Kingdom in 2016 by
Shearsman Books Ltd
50 Westons Hill Drive
Emersons Green
BRISTOL
BS16 7DF

Shearsman Books Ltd Registered Office
30–31 St. James Place, Mangotsfield, Bristol BS16 9JB
(this address not for correspondence)

ISBN 978-1-84861-460-4
First Edition

CONTENTS

Introduction

ROBERT HAMPSON

This collection of reminiscences owes an immense debt to Geraldine Monk's *Cusp*, which constructs a "collective autobiography" of poets "living and writing in England and Wales" in the 1960s and 1970s "away from those two strongholds of poetic power", Cambridge and London.[1] It was also prompted by an interview (involving Ken Edwards and myself) with Sophie Seita about *Alembic*, which made us realise just how much we had forgotten since Wolfgang Görtschacher's interviews with us in the 1990s.[2] In the background also is *The Grand Piano*, the multivolume "experiment in collective autobiography", published serially between 2006 and 2010 about San Francisco poetry.[3] *CLASP* is an exercise in collective remembering – with, as Lawrence Upton's essay suggests, a consciousness of memory work as also a process of selecting, forgetting and inventing. The original plan had been to focus on the 1970s, the decade during which we had co-edited *Alembic* with Peter Barry. Some of those we approached felt they could not usefully remember enough of their poetry activities in this period; some were reluctant to return to the past.[4] Also, as the project developed, it became clear that the original plan wouldn't work: the history did not fit neatly into the limits of the decade. We would have to start earlier to understand the roots of 1970s London poetry, and we would have to stray into the 1980s to see how some of the debates and actions of the 1970s played out.

We might as well begin here, then, with London in the late 1960s as viewed from the Strand. The US is engaged in war in Vietnam, and there are massive anti-war demonstrations world-wide. In London, there are battles outside the US Embassy in Grosvenor Square, and Fleet Street is still boarded up on Monday mornings after the weekend demonstrations.[5] At this time, Fleet Street was still the centre of the newspaper industry: the battle of Wapping, when News International would take on the print unions, had to wait for the election of the Thatcher government at the end of the following decade. There are pubs in Fleet Street and off the Strand where women are not allowed to buy a drink. Third-year male students in the Skeat Library are clean-cut, clean-shaven, dressed in sports jackets and grey flannel trousers; first-years are long-haired and moustachioed, wearing army-surplus great-coats. Meanwhile, elsewhere, students are occupying the Sorbonne and, much closer to home, the LSE; while visiting students bring news of the SDS's struggles in Germany.

As Robert Hewison has argued, the cultural revolution of the Sixties in London was the product of two ideologies developing in parallel: "the affluent and hedonistic Sixties of 'Swinging London', and the oppositional culture of the underground".[6] There were various signs of this developing oppositional culture throughout the sixties. Hewison dates the start from the contributions made by William Burroughs and Alexander Trocchi to the 1962 Edinburgh Writers Conference organised by John Calder.[7] In London, the public emergence of this culture was at the first International Festival of Poetry held at the Albert Hall in June 1965 – organised at a week's notice, in response to Allen Ginsberg's presence in London, with Trocchi as MC – which brought in 7,000 people for a four-hour poetry reading.[8] However, this legendary event was not created *ex nihilo*, but can rather be seen as the outcome of some years of public poetry readings by Michael Horovitz, and other London-based British poets such as Pete Brown and Spike Hawkins.[9] In September 1966, *The Destruction in Art Symposium* brought event-art to London: Gustav Metzger's auto-destructive art; Herman Nitsch and the Viennese Institute for Direct Art; Wolf Vostell and other Fluxus artists; and sound poetry from Bob Cobbing and Henri Chopin.[10] Gustav Metzger's student, Pete Townsend, was to take destructive art to a wider audience, while the Fluxus artist Yoko Ono, who came over to London to perform her 'Cut Piece' at the Symposium, was also to have an impact on popular culture. Perhaps most important, during July 1967, *The Dialectics of Liberation* conference took place at the Round House, Chalk Farm. This was a coming together of artists, anti-psychiatrists, activists and philosophers, including Julian Beck of the New York Living Theatre, Allen Ginsberg, R.D. Laing and David Cooper, Stokely Carmichael and Black Power, John Gerassi and Ernest Mandel, Paul Goodman and Lucien Goldman, Herbert Marcuse and Gregory Bateson. As Miles suggests, this event, organised by Laing, could be seen as "a prototype for the occupations and teach-ins that occurred during the Events of May in Paris in 1968", but its more immediate and undeniable outcome was the founding of the short-lived Anti-University of London in Rivington Street, Shoreditch.[11] The steering committee for the Anti-University included the poetry publishers Asa Benveniste and Stuart Montgomery, and the poet Ed Dorn; while the course-leaders included Bob Cobbing, Jeff Nuttall, Barry Miles, Lee Harwood and Cornelius Cardew. However, from this distance, what is remarkable about the conference is the bringing into dialogue of Black Power, revolutionary Marxism, ecology, performance art and poetry.[12] What is also noticeable is the absence of feminism: the Women's Movement was to develop more fully in the 1970s.[13] Nevertheless, here were clear signs of a politically radical, intellectually curious counter-culture.

The institutions which supported this developing counter-culture included the Institute for Contemporary Arts in Dover Street, where Horovitz's *Live New Departures* appeared regularly from 1964 to 1966, and where Anne Lauterbach subsequently set up a lecture series, *Poetry Information*, and the Arts Lab in Drury Lane, established by Jim Haynes, which ran from 1967 to 1969.[14] For the poets in this volume, the other significant phenomenon was a number of independent book-shops such as Indica Books on Kingsway, Better Books in Charing Cross Road, Bernard Stone's Turret Books in Kensington and Compendium in Camden Town, which not only provided access to books and magazines, but also acted as centres for information-exchange and making contacts. In addition, there were certain key individuals from the 1960s who had a major impact on London poetry of the 1970s. The most important of these was Bob Cobbing – founder of the Hendon Experimental Art Club in 1951 and Writers Forum and the Association of Little Presses during the 1960s – who was manager of Better Books in the late 1960s.[15] Another was Jeff Nuttall. Inspired by William Burroughs's work with cut-ups and fold-ins, Nuttall had begun publishing *My Own Mag: A Superabsorbent Periodical* in November 1963. ("The message was: if you want to exist you must accept the flesh and the moment.")[16] In 1964, he received a copy of Alexander Trocchi's *Sigma Portfolio* and linked up with Trocchi's situationist-inspired project of cultural revolution.[17] In 1966, he also began to work with the *People Show*, a kind of Dada cabaret, which he stayed with till he moved to Bradford at the end of 1968. Both Sigma and the People Show staged events in the Better

Books basement. Nuttall's *Bomb Culture* (1968) provided an essential guide to post-war culture for those coming of age in the 1970s through its linkage of radical art and radical politics.[18]

The standard story of London innovative poetry of the 1970s is dominated by events at the Poetry Society between 1971 and 1977. This was the period when the mainstream of modernist poetries reached a higher public visibility through readings at the Poetry Society and in the pages of *Poetry Review* under Eric Mottram's editorship. Peter Barry has written about these events in his book *Poetry Wars*, and, inevitably, the Poetry Society features in a number of the reminiscences in this volume – primarily as a hub of activities, a congenial meeting place and a source of information about contemporary poetries.[19] However, that narrative conceals other areas of poetic activity in London in the 1970s. Mottram, for example, besides editing *Poetry Review* and teaching full-time at King's College, London, was also involved in a series of large-scale conferences on contemporary poetry at the Polytechnic of Central London, as well as organising smaller-scale one-day conferences on contemporary US poetry at the institute for United States Studies. Bob Cobbing's Writers Forum ran continuously through this period – either in the Poetry Society or outside it. In addition, Cobbing, who had been involved in setting up the Association of Little Presses, whose annual meetings became an important event in the innovative poet's social calendar, established the Poets Conference, a trade union for poets, dedicated to setting a minimum wage for poetry readings.[20] He was also involved with founding the Film-makers Co-op and the London Musicians Collective, both of which had porous boundaries with the London experimental poetry groupings.

Indeed, as this collection of reminiscences makes clear, there were various poetry groupings that could be included under the heading of London experimental or innovative poetry. There were not just divisions between page-based, sound, visual and performance poetries – although some poets, like Allen Fisher or Ulli McCarthy, covered all these areas. There were also outliers like Bernard Kelly's Dadaist group around the Enterprise pub in Chalk Farm, Carlyle Reedy in Notting Hill or Jeremy Reed. The attempt to present a "London School" of innovative poetry is also complicated by the fact that London was (and is) a place of transit.

As many of these reminiscences show, few of the poets (with the striking exception of Allen Fisher) were actually born in London. Many of the reminiscences are stories of arrival and, often, passing through. The Paladin Re/Active Anthology of "3 London Poets", which published work by Allen Fisher, Bill Griffiths and Brian Catling, was, significantly and prophetically, entitled *future exiles*.[21] An anthology of "new poets from London", *Floating Capital* (1991), began with work by Cobbing and Fisher to acknowledge their importance for the younger poets included, but, though the collection accurately represents the London poetry of the 1980s, it is interesting that neither of the editors and none of the younger contributors now live in London.[22] The "London School" turns out to be diasporic. However, there were various reading series (of varying longevity) that provided a focus during the 1970s: short-run series like Zero Events and Future Events; longer running reading series like King's Readings and Sub-Voicive. In addition, there were also workshops – such as the Translation Workshop at King's College, RASP (run collectively by Paul Brown, Ken Edwards and Allen Fisher), and Robert Sheppard's Thursday evening meetings at his home in Tooting Bec – which functioned as assembly points and growth points for London poets.

London poetry of the 1970s was rhizomatic in its organisation. It grew out of a 1960s spirit of self-determination that included both a form-breaking freedom and a concern for ownership of the means of production. Publication through small presses and little magazines was a conscious choice: self-publishing included greater control over both content and presentation. There were also interactions with other art forms: an openness to poetic experimentation was combined with an interest in performance, sound and visual poetics. There was also an engagement with poetry at an international level. At the same time, there was an awareness of other related practices more locally: the Essex School around Wivenhoe Park, for example, or activities in Cambridge such as the publications of Rod Mengham's Equipage Press and the annual CCCP. Larry Lynch has written that "The idea of practice... as the object of sustained critical attention, was an informal proposition at Cambridge".[23] In London, by comparison, there was an interest in a mapping of the field of poetic practices but without "sustained critical attention". Indeed, there was, rather, a marked reluctance to voice critical positions.

In his book *In the Sixties*, Miles observes that art college was, for him, "a stepping stone out of the... working-class".[24] For some of the contributors to the present volume, university had the same function. After the 1963 Robbins Report, which accepted the principle that higher education was the right of anyone whose ability merited it, the population of the universities doubled in the 1960s. At the same time, there was a brief window when the working-classes could escape from the idea that certain areas of culture were banned to them. Instead, the field of culture was open and, as many of these reminiscences show, the boundaries were porous. The later concern with "elitism" has had the effect of closing off those areas from the working-class again. The disappearance of independent bookshops and the closure of public libraries has removed important points of access to a wider culture. On the other hand, the internet and digital media have made documentation and communication faster and easier.

Notes

[1] Geraldine Monk (ed.), *Cusp: Recollections of Poetry in Transition* (Bristol: Shearsman Books, 2012). I am also personally indebted to Geraldine for her advice about handling such a volume of "recollections".

[2] Sophie Seita, 'Interview with Ken Edwards and Robert Hampson', *Mimeo Mimeo* 9 (April 2014), pp. 45-65; Wolfgang Görtschacher, 'Interview with Ken Edwards: From *Alembic* to Reality Street Editions' and 'Interview with Robert Hampson: Exploring Different Forms and Formats' in Wolfgang Görtschacher, *Contemporary Views on the Little Magazine Scene* (Salzburg: Poetry Salzburg, 2000), pp. 233-264 and 388-426.

[3] Rae Armantrout, Steve Benson, Carla Harryman, Lyn Hejinian, Tom Mandel, Ted Pearson, Kit Robinson, Ron Silliman, Bob Perelman, Barrett Watten, *The Grand Piano* (Detroit, mode A, 2006-10).

[4] Allen Fisher had already engaged in an act of remembering his entry into poetry in the 1960s. See 'Skipping across the pond: interactions between American and British poetries 1964-1970' in David Nowell Smith and Abigail Lang (eds), *The Legacy of Modernism* (2015).

[5] The Vietnam Solidarity Committee, headed by Tariq Ali, organised a demonstration outside the US Embassy on 17 March 1968. The police sealed off the square and then attacked the crowds with repeated charges on horseback.

[6] Robert Hewison, *Too Much: Art and Society in the Sixties 1960-75* (London: Methuen, 1986), p. xiii.

[7] Burroughs was based in London from 1965 to 1974.

[8] There have been many accounts of this event. See, for example, Barry Miles, *London Calling: a Countercultural History of London since 1945* (London: Atlantic Books, 2010), pp.144-53.

[9] In 1959, Michael Horovitz had launched his magazine *New Departures* in Oxford with the first issue featuring work by Samuel Beckett, Burroughs and Kurt Schwitters. He subsequently teamed up with Pete Brown, and, from 1960 onwards, as *Live New Departures*, hitch-hiked around Britain giving readings in colleges, pubs and art-galleries in a jazz-and-poetry format, linking up with poets in Liverpool, Edinburgh and Newcastle. In Liverpool, Adrian Henri and Johnny Byrne started holding poetry readings in Streate's Coffee-Bar from 1961. Tom and Connie Pickard opened the Modern Tower Poetry Centre in Newcastle in 1964.

[10] Miles, pp. 153-58. It was organised by Gustav Metzger and John Sharkey; the honorary committee included Bob Cobbing, Jim Haynes, Barry Miles, and Wolf Vostell.

[11] Miles, p. 257, p. 258. Cornelius Cardew taught experimental music; Bob Cobbing taught sound poetry; Lee Harwood and Ed Dorn were also involved.

[12] Stokely Carmichael was a dominant figure at the conference. Robin Bunce dates the 1970s explosion of black power within the UK to this event: within a week of the conference the United Coloured People's Association had expelled its white members and produced a new black-power oriented manifesto; within a year, there was a British Black Panther movement. See Robin Bunce and Paul Field, *Darcus Howe: A Political Biography* (London: Bloomsbury, 2013).

[13] Hewison notes that, in 1969, "a loose federation of women's groups had begun to evolve into the London Workshop" and that a conference at Ruskin College, Oxford, in February 1970, was "the first national conference of the women's liberation movement" (p. 217). Carolee Schneemann performed at DIAS and the feminist Juliet Mitchell was, however, a member of the steering committee of the Anti-University.

[14] The ICA was set up in 1946 by Roland Penrose, Herbert Read and Geoffrey Grigson. Both Penrose and Read had backgrounds in surrealism: they had organised the London International Surrealist Exhibition of 1936.

[15] Writers Forum's first publication, *Limbless Virtuoso*, by Keith Musgrave and Jeff Nuttall, appeared in 1963.

[16] Jeff Nuttall, *Bomb Culture* (London: Paladin, 1970), p. 141. As Nuttall ob-

serves, "we were in the same place but Burroughs was travelling in the opposite direction" (p.142).

[17] Hewison, p.107-9. According to Miles, Nuttall subsequently did all the mimeograph printing for Trocchi, turning out 39 pamphlets over three years on the school duplicating machine he shared with Cobbing. Barry Miles, *London Calling*, pp. 137, 139.

[18] Jeff Nuttall, *Bomb Culture* (London: Paladin, 1970).

[19] Peter Barry, *Poetry Wars: British Poetry of the 1970s and the Battle of Earls Court* (Cambridge: Salt, 2006).

[20] For a fuller account of Cobbing's role and activities, See Stephen Willey, , 'Bob Cobbing 1950-1978: Performance Poetry and the Institution', Unpublished PhD Thesis (University of London, 2013).

[21] *Future exiles: 3 London Poets* (London: Paladin, 1992).

[22] Adrian Clarke & Robert Sheppard (eds), *Floating Capital: new poets from London* (Elmwood, Connecticut: Potes & Poets Press, 1991). Of the poets included, Gilbert Adair and cris cheek now live in the USA; Hazel Smith lives in Australia; Paul Brown, Adrian Clarke, and Ken Edwards have moved to the south coast; and Robert Sheppard and Maggie O'Sullivan have moved north.

[23] Larry Lynch, Foreword to John Hall, *On Performance Writing* (Bristol: Shearsman Books, 2013), p.15.

[24] Barry Miles, *In the Sixties* (London: Jonathan Cape, 2002), 5.

Challenging the "Little England" Consensus in British Poetry: Eric Mottram, *Poetry Review* and *Talus*

CLIVE BUSH

Eric Mottram burst onto the academic scene in the UK in 1961, with teaching in Singapore and Holland behind him, and accompanied by a *Times* fourth leader noting the oddity of the fact of American literature being taught in England. A Cold War freebie got him to America in 1960 at the U.S. government's expense where he met new poets, among them Ginsberg, Williams, Olson and experienced the end of the classic jazz era in St Louis, Chicago and New York. He brought a recently acquired knowledge of American poetry like cultural dynamite into a dead and decaying English culture.

Today poets of my generation are "accused" of being influenced by American poets. From the sixties onwards we were delighted to have been so. Auden, Isherwood, Spender, Larkin *et al* were all dead ends for us. They could be safely left to the reactionary British media and East Coast Ivy League professors with their "English" tweed jackets.

The new American oxygen flowed in through a number of people, including Prynne and Andrew Crozier, but Mottram was the most ubiquitous and most energetic. He made us read Whitman, Emily Dickinson, Pound, Eliot (as an American poet, not as a nativized supporter of Anthony Eden's Conservative Party), William Carlos Williams, Mina Loy, H.D., Hart Crane, Muriel Rukeyser, Robert Duncan, the Beats, Charles Olson, Jonathan Williams, Clayton Eshleman, Jerome Rothenberg, Anne Waldman, Denise Levertov, George Oppen, Lorine Niedecker and many others. But the critics were and are wrong to say that the American influence was dominant. Mottram had a powerful connection with continental Europe having taught in Groningen University, where almost like intellectually adventurous 17th-century Holland, new European directions in poetry, painting, film and contemporary classical music had been, unlike in Britain, warmly welcomed during the 1950s.

In 1971 for a brief moment Mottram and the sound poet Bob Cobbing took over the highly conservative Poetry Society and *Poetry*

Review. The establishment speedily took its revenge, but the intervening period of four or five years opened up new worlds of poetry to the British public. Already in the first issue of Mottram's *Poetry Review* in the Autumn of 1971, new young English poets and somewhat more established American poets shared the stage. On the English side were the poets the establishment chose to ignore: Lee Harwood, Allen Fisher, Stuart Montgomery, Jeff Nuttall, Paul Evans, Val Warner, Roy Fisher, and Gael Turnbull. Robert Duncan, Michael McClure, Muriel Rukeyser, and Gilbert Sorrentino were well-established American poets, but they were published alongside their younger English contemporaries. At the back of the issue there was a section called 'Poetry Information' which gave good summarizing, highly detailed bibliographical information on each of the poets.

As we look back we can see Mottram's touch was sure. Lee Harwood and Allen Fisher are now well-represented in a number of collections.[1] Paul Evans most sadly died young, and still needs a serious collection. Nuttall's poetry was only part of his huge creativity in painting, jazz performances, cartoons and street performance art. Val Warner has had a distinguished career at Carcanet and her work is collected by that press.[2] Roy Fisher was amazingly taken up by Oxford University Press, though his superb work is hardly better known for that.[3] As for the Americans, Robert Duncan was one of the greatest Californian poets, breaking through on the threshold of general recognition at the time, though the American East Coast literary establishment have always ignored him: the latest squib being Robert Baird's snotty review of Lisa Jarnot's *Robert Duncan: The Ambassador from Venus* in the *London Review of Books*.[4] Muriel Rukeyser in her last decade provided serious links with the American leftist 1930s as well as with West Coast poetry traditions. She died in 1980 but is only now being seriously studied and has only relatively recently been provided with a comprehensive and reliable *Collected Poems*.[5]

In 1987 Shamoon Zamir, a graduate student of Mottram's and the young Norwegian poet, Hanne Bramness, started *Talus*, equipped with contacts generously provided by Mottram, and more than ably assisted by Stephen Want and Marzia Balzani. In many ways it was a continuation of the spirit of Mottram's *Poetry Review* but it contained essays and interviews in addition to poetry, and the first issue signalled the international range. The first issue had an interview with Clayton Eshleman by the Hungarian poet Gyula Kodolanyi (currently editor of *The Hungarian Review*), a sizeable poem by Amiri Baraka, an extract by Iain Sinclair from his forthcoming novel *White Chappell, Scarlet Tracings* (Paladin, 1988), poems by Clark Coolidge, Jeff Nuttall, Anselm Hollo, Anne Waldman, Pierre Joris, Douglas Oliver, a short prose piece by Johanna Drucker and possibly Mottram's best essay: 'Out of sight but never out of mind: Fears of Invasion in American Culture', which he had given some seven years earlier as a plenary lecture at the first American Studies Conference to be held in Budapest during the Cold War. I was present at that charged political moment and it had been greeted with rapturous and thunderous applause. A new, sophisticated generation was growing up, casting a suspicious eye on ideologues of East and West alike. *Talus* slowly developed away from the Mottram list though still in the same spirit. Jacqueline Kaye wrote on the *The Song of Roland, The Poem of the Cid* and *The Lusiads,* looking at the cultural palimpsests and erasures of literary epics which signalled the emergence of nationalistic "Europe" from its Christian and Muslim roots. Hanne Bramness ensured that Scandinavian poetry entered the frame. Work by Inger Elisabeth Hansen, Rune Christiansen, Erling Indreeide, Terje Johansse, Torgeir Schjerven, Thor Sørheim, Thorvald Steen was published. For the first time a Moroccan poet, Abdellatif Laabi, a Pakistani writer, Zmiruddin Ahmad, and a native American, Duane Niatum, were published. More Algerian and Moroccan writers appeared: Rachid Boudjedra, Mohammed Essergini, Mohammed Khaïr-Eddine. The Tunisian writer Abdelwahab was published along with Gu Cheng, one of the young Chinese poets of the new democracy movement of 1979. The support of new British poets continued through this expansion. Bill Griffiths, Allen Fisher, Bob Cobbing, Thomas A. Clark, Gilbert Adair, cris cheek, David Miller, Ulli Freer, Tom Raworth, Gavin Selerie, Lawrence Upton were all published. It was a true extension of the Mottram spirit which had moved beyond Europe and America.

In this necessarily brief account a quick review of his exchange of letters with Robert Duncan at the time of *Poetry Review* thickens the always difficult question of cultural and political exchange. The emphasis here is on reciprocity. Mottram explained to Duncan that he wanted the *Review* to represent the best in English and American poetry together. In some ways it had more than a touch of 1945 about it. Mottram's enthusiasm for American literature was everywhere apparent and the letters reveal the constant attacks on Mottram from *TLS* and others for contaminating the little-England traditions. But Mottram also dissented from some aspects of the livelier cultural dogmatisms of an already fading sixties American scene. Clayton Eshleman's *Caterpillar* whose earlier issues had contained parts of Duncan's *H.D. Book*, essays by Norman O. Brown, and stills from Carolee Schneeman's *Fuses* came under leftist fire from Mottram's scepticism. It had deteriorated into "priesthood and dogma".[6] That was Mottram's comment on Shamanistic, cult-ridden California. He was right but it was more complex than that. There was a sense that, as Tariq Ali has recently said of Stuart Hall, Mottram didn't quite "get" the sixties.[7] That is to say its best and more liberating aspects. But its worst aspects were very transparent to someone on the left who had had gone through the depression, served in the Second World War, and took socialism seriously. He unburdened himself to Duncan about the "grim playboys of the Yippies, the repetitions of The New Left and the separatisms of the Karengists [Black nationalist ideologues]" (46). It took many years before identity politics was even questioned in the United States. Only now, forty years on, is there beginning a more serious political-economic investigation of a hundred-year alliance between Presidential and Banking power which has undermined the sovereignty of elected governments.[8]

Mottram equally drew Duncan's attention to the politics of the British scene, the rise of a distracting celebrity-oriented media, the rising living costs, censorship over Northern Ireland, the Orwellian lying of the phrase "peace-keeping force", the "old capitalist shit of keeping workers in bad conditions of housing and labour while the profits leave the country" (57). Duncan acknowledged similar conditions in America, after all he had "come out" in Dwight Macdonald's politics in 1944, and had very much more than a touch of American thirties leftism in his make-up. He would agree with Mottram's insistence on "class" analysis (67).

The correspondence is revealing, too, of much of Mottram's attitude to flip American fashionable punditry. While admiring Zukofsky he severely criticized his thrown-off "What use is Coleridge?", saying it was "pure New York" (77). He also felt Zukofsky too mechanistic: he was never convinced that the "*Matthew Passion* really got into his body, and justified his usage of it" (77).

That sense of the body was also to sow the seeds of Mottram's radical ecological instincts. Not only did he quote Duncan Lynn Townsend White's famous essay, 'The Historical Roots of our Ecological Crisis', "By destroying pagan animism, Christianity made it possible to exploit nature in a mood of indifference to the feelings of natural objects,"[9] but his work showed also the influence of Hans Jonas, the Frankfurt School philosopher and theologian, critical of Heidegger, who used the power of the critical philosophic tradition to re-orientate thoughts of our relation to the natural world, including death.[10]

In early 1974 Duncan sent Mottram a present of his *A Seventeenth Century Suite in Homage to the Metaphysical Genius in English Poetry*[11] in recognition of the strength of the tradition of English poetry. Years later Mottram's last letter to Duncan, 1986, noted: "Our British Poetry scene—the unofficial one—strives and thrives—against grim odds" (149). It still does.

NOTES

[1] See, for example, Lee Harwood, *Collected Poems 1964-2004* (Shearsman, 2004) and Allen Fisher, *Place* (Reality Street, 2005).

[2] See, for example, Val Warner, *Under the Penthouse* (Carcanet, 1973) or *Before Lunch* (Carcanet, 1986).

[3] See, for example, Roy Fisher, *Poems 1955-1987* (Oxford University Press, 1988).

[4] Robert Baird, 'Use Use Use' a review of Lisa Jarnot's *Robert Duncan: The Ambassador from Venus. London Review of Books*, Vol. 35 No. 20, 24 October 2013, pages 29-31.

[5] Janet E. Kaufman and Anne F. Herzog (eds), *The Collected Poems of Muriel Rukeyser* (Pittsburgh: University of Pittsburgh Press, 2005).

[6] Amy Evans and Shamoon Zamir (eds), *The Unruly Garden: Robert Duncan and Eric Mottram, Letters and Essays* (Oxford et al.: Peter Lang, 1995), p. 43. Further references to this work follow in the text.

[7] Suzi Weissman interviews Tariq Ali on Stuart Hall, on 'Beneath the Surface'. Radio Interview 14 February, 2014, on KPFK 90.7fm LA, 98.7fm Santa Barbara, 93.7fm N. San Diego.

[8] Exemplary in this regard is Nomi Prins's magnificent, *All the Presidents' Bankers: The Hidden Alliances that Drive American Power* (New York: Nation Books, 2014). Away from the half-radicalism of "race-and-gender" American Studies wallahs, serious political and economic power critiques are developing. One thinks of Susan George's pioneering *A Fate Worse than Debt*, 1988, and Naomi Klein's *The Shock Doctrine*, 2007, while the sidelined Noam Chomsky has been harrying the State Department for decades.

[9] Lynn Townsend White Jr., 'The Historical Roots of Our Ecologic Crisis', *Science*, vol. 155, no. 3767 (10 March 1967), 1203-1207.

[10] Mottram lent me (highly recommended) Hans Jonas's *Philosophical Essays: from Ancient Creed to Technological Man* (Chicago and London: University of Chicago Press, 1974) when I had a long discussion with him about the conclusion of my book *Halfway to Revolution: Investigations and crisis in the work of Henry Adams, William James and Gertrude Stein* (New Haven and London, Yale University Press, 1991) sometime in 1990. I think Jonas's thinking was important for Mottram in helping him to revise his thoughts about critical philosophy and dialectic in general with more field-oriented ecological issues.

[11] This was privately printed in San Francisco in 1974 and finally appeared in Robert Duncan's *Ground Work Before the War* (New York: A New Directions Book, 1984), pp. 70-93.

In the Poetry Zones

Paul A. Green

My discovery at seventeen of the Feldman/Gartenberg anthology
Protest (Ginsberg, Burroughs, Kerouac, Rexroth etc) plus the Jazz-
Poetry edition of Mike Horovitz's *New Departures* first encouraged me
to explore the poetry zones as an active participant – with my mate
Vincent Crane who played blues piano. At a New Departures gig at
the Ben Uri Gallery in late 1962 Horovitz and Pete Brown read, Bobby
Wellins played with Stan Tracey – and in the interval I read my latest
schoolgirl-crush poem over Vincent's walking bass. Anselm Hollo, the
other poet on the bill, was very kind about it.

So the British Beats were my roots, while performance, with music/
mixed media elements, was as much a focus as the little mags of the
time like *Underground* or *I Like You*, which published poets like Lee
Harwood and Adrian Mitchell.[1] At Oxford and London around 1965-
66 Iain Stewart and I staged events under the banner of 'The Word
Engine', featuring Vincent's band plus guests such as Pete Brown and
Libby Houston, as well as our own efforts, declaimed against Hammond
organ and honking saxes.

Pete Brown's encouragement led me to join a troupe of poets
scrabbling on the Fringe of the Edinburgh Festival. We eyed each
other up warily in the bar of the Traverse Theatre. Nevertheless, Pete
negotiated amiably between the various poetic factions vying for slots,
balancing the territorial claims of the native Scots, like the veteran
Marxist Hugh McDiarmid, still celebrating "the eternal lightning
of Lenin's bones", against a massed insurgency from the Children
of Albion, represented by Ted Milton, Spike Hawkins and Libby
Houston, the Mersey Sound (Brian Patten, Roger McGough) and
the acid prophet Paolo Leonni. I was there with my friend Delaney
from London, not so much a poet, more a stream-of-consciousness
stand-up ranter, firing off gags about nuclear bunkers interspersed
with Fenian ballads, so my faux-Ginsbergian theatrics were juxtaposed
with Delaney's energetic renditions of 'The Wearing of the Green'. This
random eclecticism seems typical of the "alternative" poetry-reading
culture of the time, when disparate rebels were drawn together in a

common alliance against an academic and/or political consensus that had marginalised them.

From 1968 to 1972 I was in Vancouver, initially on the Creative Writing program at University of British Columbia and subsequently scuffling around as freelance writer/broadcaster. The Canadian West Coast had its own tribal clusterings. The UBC Creative Writing department, under the influence of J. Michael Yates, favoured European High Modernism, especially a kind of icy-eyed surrealism in the mode of Karl Krolow, while the UBC English Department had more affinity with the Black Mountain school and with concrete experimentation, typified by their invitation to Jackson Mac Low, whom I interviewed for local radio. I recall excellent readings by John Robert Colombo, Robert Sward, George Amabile and Michael Bullock, among others, but all in formal campus lecture room settings. My own practice now veered more towards the recording studio, exploiting the possibilities of vocal treatments, electronic sound and the mixing desk, to create tapes for black-room immersion or full-frontal rock PA assault. Lawrence Russell at the University of Victoria championed this kind of work in his pioneering tape magazine *DNA*; and we continue to collaborate digitally today – via www.culturecourt.com. However, my contact with the mutating UK/London scene was inevitably limited and this sense of isolation continued when I returned to England, where I somehow ended up in Torquay.

The nearest node of poetic activity was Dartington, where John Hall organised readings, notably a fine rendition of *Place* by Allen Fisher. At my Torquay college I presented, among others, Ken Smith, who edited *The South West Review* out of Exeter, and Vivienne Finch, who ran *Tangent* magazine and organised her own reading series 'Grundy' at a small theatre in Kingston – I believe Yann Lovelock and Ian Robinson may have read there.[2] Vivienne, like Ken Smith and Ian Robinson, is sadly dead, and I haven't been able to glean more information. However, I did a performance there in 1975. Ken Edwards reviewed it, describing me as "a short bearded bloke in a white suit with a Beefheartian manner" which I construed as a great compliment. Correspondence with Ken and Vivienne was effectively my lifeline to the poetry community outside Devon, apart from magazines like *Little Word Machine*, *Oasis* and *Alembic*.[3] Ken's *Reality Studios* introduced me to the $L=A=N=G=U=A=G=E$ writers, while reading with him at the Spacex Gallery in Exeter steered me towards new compositional approaches, according to my 1980 notebook: "*Tilth* works by totally opening to flux and controlling it by denying controls..."[4] With Vivienne, I made contact with Iain Sinclair, Allen Fisher and Lee Harwood, as we planned our ill-fated project on the theme of "Place" for BBC Radio 3. Only one programme was completed in its entirety – Iain Sinclair's *Lud Heat* which combined readings with guided tours through Ripper alleys and the bowels of Hawksmoor churches. Officially it was axed because of technical issues – a disparity between the high quality binaural location recordings and the lower-fi interview clips – but I suspect the concept, both in theme and execution, was just too weird for the BBC bureaucrats, still moulded by a post-Leavisite literary culture.

Returning to London in 1982 I encountered more divergence, between an emergent "performance poetry", exemplified by the Apples and Snakes collective, which was to evolve into slam and/or comedy routines, and the world of "linguistically innovative poetries". Attempts were still made to create an interzone, as in the extraordinary Angels of Fire Festival at the Cockpit Theatre in November 1983. In the course of a week, one could – to take a small random sample – hear punk ranters, the sibylline tones of David Gascoyne, feminist workshops on the poetics of motherhood, Lol Coxhill, Bill Griffiths, video by Jez Welsh (who later recruited me to the Quantum Brothers), cris cheek in a dance called 'Talking Turkey', dialect poets like Valerie Bloom and John Agard, poets with neo-romantic aspirations like the Festival instigator Jay Ramsay, and people who had apparently walked in off the street to share their mental health issues. It was an exhausting marathon – I was there helping with sound most nights – but its chaos was exhilarating.

Around the same period I was frequently attending the Sub-Voicive sessions arranged by Gilbert Adair and Patricia Farrell at the White Swan in Covent Garden. The upper room was dark and claustrophobic, with a strange masonic ambience, adorned with crude reproductions of old masters – yet the incongruity of the setting only increased one's sense of conspiratorial subversion. One kept fragmentary notes. "turbulent word humps bump out of his mouth" (20/03/83 re cris cheek) and "rising from the back of the room the plump silvery form of Bob Cobbing"

(10/05/83). The social bonding was important – "so where's that nice jolly girlfriend of yours?" (08/11/83 from Eric Mottram). Most of the audience knew each other, but sometimes strangers infiltrated. During my reading on October 4, 1983, a man let out an involuntary cry of alarm. He had never been to a poetry event before and thought he had blundered into some sinister seance.

Another venue was the London Musicians Collective in a former British Rail canteen in Camden, which hosted the New River Project, an ongoing enterprise inspired, like so many, by Bob Cobbing. The day Vincent and I performed there, Allen Fisher and Paige Mitchell were doing live painting, Maggie O'Sullivan was reading and Bird Yak (Clive Fencott, Hugh Metcalfe and Cobbing) were performing. As I recall, Bruce Andrews and Sally Silver did a poetry/dance performance there, but the details are hazy.

South London was less well served with innovative poetry. In the mid-eighties Ken Edwards tried to redress the balance with the RASP series, a collaboration between Reality Street, Paul Brown's Actual Size Press and Allen Fisher's *Spanner* at a community centre in Balfour Street. Brown, Fisher, Iain Sinclair, Brian Catling, Lawrence Upton, Adrian Clarke and Johan de Wit were among those who read there. It was a small venue – a "community room" – but I have a distinct memory that it was pretty full that evening. One night, however, Crane and Green played to an audience of two, who escaped at the interval, an episode which typifies the challenges of building an audience for poetry.

By the late eighties, I was becoming more preoccupied with speculative fiction, audio drama and my collaborations with video artist Jeremy Welsh as The Quantum Brothers, which evolved into the video poem series *The Slow Learning*. But in retrospect I recognise the stimulus and sense of community I received from this quasi-underground culture of gatherings in dingy function rooms, which could suddenly become zones of amazement.

NOTES

[1] These were both Oxford-based magazines. *Underground*, edited by Tony Allan (an undergraduate at Corpus Christi), produced a single issue in the summer of 1966. This included poems by Lee Harwood, Adrian Mitchell, Tina Cunliffe and Dave Cunliffe (among others); an essay on anarchism by Sir Herbert Read; and a poem on Bakunin by Robert Nichols. *I Like You*, another short-lived magazine, was edited by Keith Buchan (an undergraduate at Lincoln College). It contained work by Pete Brown, Spike Hawkins, Libby Houston, Adrian Mitchell (and others), and was illustrated with psychedelic line-drawings.

[2] *Tangent* magazine was founded by Vivienne Finch (and co-edited with William Pryor). It ran from 1975 to 1981.

[3] *Little Word Machine* (1972-79) was edited by Nick Toczek, *Oasis* (1969-83, 1991-2004) by Ian Robinson, *Alembic* (1973-79) by Peter Barry, Ken Edwards and Robert Hampson.

[4] *Reality Studios* (1978-88); *Tilth* (Newcastle: Galloping Dog Press, 1980).

Back Then

JOHN WELCH

It's 1966 and I'm living in a bedsitter in North London, feeling uncomfortably isolated after three difficult years at Cambridge. I think it was a classified ad in the *New Statesman* that led me to Norman Hidden's Writers Workshop. This met once a month in a large space above a pub in Covent Garden and I became a regular. There wasn't strictly any "workshop" element. There was an invited guest reader or two, then shorter readings by "workshop members" and finally "Over to You", or "open mic" as it would be called today. It was very well-attended. There was no artistic programme as such, but there was an openness about it, and I can trace very many of my connections in the poetry world to contacts first made there. The guest readers tended to be of the mainstream variety but they were quite an eclectic bunch – I remember Edgell Rickword, a left-wing poet of the 1930s, and Tambimuttu, the editor of *Poetry London*…[1] Then one evening Donald Gardner turned up and read a poem in the "Over to You" section. Afterwards he took some of us with him to Jim Haynes's Arts Lab in Drury Lane, that epitome of the Sixties which I'd not been to before, and there was John Lennon in a white suit, paying a visit with a group of followers. Don had just set up Guerrilla Poets which met once a month here. His inspiration was New York and the Beats – there was no mention of Black Mountain that I recall. The people who turned up to read – everyone got to read one poem – were a remarkably disparate collection. It was non-judgmental in a 1960s letting it-all-hang-out sort of way, a witnessing for the faith perhaps. This openness and Don's example did encourage some freeing-up in my writing. I jibbed at the impromptu street-readings though, and Don, inspired by Julian Beck's 'Living Theatre', set up his own theatre group, before going to live in Amsterdam.

Meanwhile looking for somewhere to publish poems I had made contact with Tim Longville's *Grosseteste Review*, published some work in there and started to receive Longville's long and detailed letters.[2] But I still had no real idea where those poets he published were coming from.

In 1969 I went to France and spent a year in Lyon teaching English. It was soon after I came back that I bumped into the poet Anthony Howell again – we'd first met at Norman Hidden's Workshop. Anthony was on the point, you might say, of being "included". His first collection, *Inside the Castle*, had been "well-received".[3] But now he had discovered Ashbery, at that time not generally read, and not published, in this country. Anthony was interested in such things as random or arbitrary procedures used to generate texts, in something he later called "abstract poetry". He told me he was starting a Workshop. I went round to the Hampstead flat where he lived with Signe, his Norwegian partner. (Michel Couturier, a French structuralist poet and critic and regular participant at the workshop couldn't get over this name – Anthony, married to the sign!) I showed Anthony some work. He sat opposite me reading the poems, squaring up to them and every so often emitting a deep sigh. His criticisms were frank, abrupt and startling. There was something bracing about it though.

You could say that I, along with some others, had been recruited and for the several months that the workshop carried on – it met once a week – it was intense. Not that everyone who came had signed up to Anthony's agenda, and there were many who just dropped in for the odd session. But for me the experience was a release. I felt poems could be made out of all kinds of specialist vocabularies. You opened dictionaries, textbooks and words fell out. Perhaps it was like re-living the excitements of modernism, this feeling that anything was possible. After the session we would go and have a curry and then I would walk home – I had a bedsitter in Kilburn, and I remember striding along in the summer night, down the hill under the huge trees, past big silent houses, back to my room. At a reading once a poet read two lines of Hafiz that he'd translated and used as an epigraph: "The book of grief is closed. It is the night of power." That was how it felt. Word-power. My room had a balcony from where I could look down towards Kilburn High Road. I was writing unrhymed sonnets at the time.[4] The arbitrariness of the form functioned as a sort of shadowy container and looking out over the city I imagined I might contain it all. For several months I existed in this shared verbal exaltation. There was no formal critical apparatus, in contrast to what had been happening in Cambridge, though I would say that Anthony did have a strong sense of what was wrong with "most poems", and a recognition of the sheer arbitrariness of the act.

It's not just the Workshop. We are going to be a movement. Anthony has invited everyone down for a week to his mother's place in Hampshire. People bring tents and come and go as they like. It's like a good-humoured holiday camp, an improvised festival with painters installing work in the fields, poets reading, performance pieces. Everyone joins in quite spontaneously. One of the artists has put up a structure of bamboo canes and threads, 'Device for Looking at Landscape' – you peer at the surrounding country framed by these structures. Her husband has covered a whole field with cardboard boxes all roughly painted with blue paint – something to do with the way they "reflect" the sky overhead. There are readings. A group of people have improvised musical instruments out of old tin cans, pieces of stick and are banging away. People dress up in odd costumes and walk slowly round in circles. And always there is the pool – the weather stays fine, and there are naked bodies diving in and out. One of the artists involved was Susan Hiller, who was working on a piece titled 'Dream Mapping'. We sat in a circle first thing in the morning sharing our dreams of the night before which were incorporated into the work. The other day at her retrospective at Tate Modern I was startled to see one of my dreams from almost forty years before, carefully framed, up there on the wall.[5]

Anthony had moved to a house in Kentish Town. A feature of his activities was always the involvement of artists, musicians, performance – in his teens he'd been a dancer with the Royal Ballet, but jibbed at its ferocious restraints. A great variety of people would drop in there. We did readings in galleries – I recall reading at Bankside in 1971, performing to Peter Logan's Mechanical Ballet. Later that year there was the 'Oz Benefit' at the ICA (Felix Dennis where are you now?).[6] This too was orchestrated by Anthony, and had to be strenuously rehearsed under his direction. There were readings, of our own work and others, but all unattributed. Marianne Faithfull read something by Herrick. I had to chant a piece of Christopher Smart while a dancer from the Ballet Rambert performed. O and there was a variety act – a man spinning plates.

In 1974 Anthony instigated *Wallpaper* magazine. This was a cooperative of ten, combining poets, visual artists and one musician, appearing in turns through the magazine's cycle. Meanwhile he was moving into Performance Art, and in that same year he founded The Theatre of Mistakes. To start with everyone joined in the Performances. There was one that took over the local street, and one in Cambridge at the 1975 poetry festival. There is something reassuring, restful even, about being made by the master of ceremonies to carry out a succession of bafflingly arbitrary actions in order to be part of some mysterious performance. But out of this coalesced a group of technically proficient and highly rehearsed performers. Was this discipline the end of the Sixties which was as much the Seventies? Was it the party where Anthony, for a bet, had someone cut off his hair.

As for our workshop, well there were plenty of other people doing it of course... There were for instance those people based in Cambridge.[7] During my time there I had overlapped with them by a year or so, but remained unaware of their existence. When I got to know their work I sometimes felt that I was someone on the outside looking in, as if there had been an explosion which bound them together and you could still just catch its echo. As for Anthony, I think he chose not to connect with them. I do recall Andrew Crozier asking me once, at a reading, "Does Anthony Howell ever show up at these events?". But, coming to all this by a roundabout route, and wanting to connect with it, in 1975 I started The Many Press.[8] You could say that this grew out of Anthony's workshop, if only because I used his golf-ball electric typewriter to typeset the first publications before doing my own paste-up and getting the pages run off at a copy centre, after which I collated, folded, stapled and trimmed them myself. This was the point of course at which mainstream publishers, one by one and with very few exceptions, stopped publishing new poetry. Starting a press like mine – and there were many others of course – had a lot to do with changes in print technology and the advent of offset litho. In real terms printing became cheaper. You could say it was demystified and in due course I was to make regular use of the Poetry Society's print shop established by Bob Cobbing. The do-it-yourself aspect was important back then, even involving at the outset presses such as Carcanet and Bloodaxe. It still feels to me very much part of the spirit of that time.

NOTES

[1] *Poetry London* ran from 1939 to 1951 and was regarded as one of the best of the period. For more on Tambimuttu, see Robert Hewison, *Under Siege: Literary Life in London 1939-45* (London: Weidenfeld and Nicolson, 1977).

[2] *Grosseteste Review* (1968-84). For a sense of the magazine's poetics, see Andrew Crozier and Tim Longville (eds), *A Various Art* (Manchester: Carcanet, 1987).

[3] Anthony Howell, *Inside the Castle* (London: The Cressett Press, 1969).

[4] Thirty of these became the first Many Press publication under the title *Six of Five* in 1975. A larger number appeared in John Welch, *Collected Poems* (Exeter: Shearsman Books, 2008).

[5] The Susan Hillier exhibition ran at Tate Britain from February 1 to May 15 2011. Its focus was on her interest in the subconscious or unconscious mind in the form of dreams, memories, or visionary experiences.

[6] *Oz*, a magazine dedicated to the revolutionary potential of sex, drugs and rock'n'roll, was first published in London in January 1967. In April 1970, *Oz* 28, a 'School Kids Issue', was put together with a group of school-children. This led to the trial of its editors – Richard Neville, Jim Anderson and Felix Dennis – charged with conspiring to corrupt young people.

[7] Andrew Crozier and Peter Riley, for example.

[8] 'Getting it Printed', my account of setting up and running The Many Press, appeared in *Jacket Magazine* 29 and can be read online at www.jacketmagazine.com

So many things

Lawrence Upton

"Ah… it seems to me,… Sorry, I've drawn a blank. Hold it. I'll have it again in a minute. I forget so many things in here, so many things."[1]

Some of us take ourselves rather seriously when we're young. In my 14th year I decided to be a poet, defined as committing oneself to write or revise verse every day, an idea I took from a TV documentary on Robert Graves. I'd start from my fourteenth birthday, I decided; at the same time, I would leave the Roman Catholic Church.

The latter might be the bigger step from my parents' point of view; I spent time preparing; but horror at eternal damnation proved less than their horror of my failing to be able to make a living.

They bought me a typewriter, seeing my need for neat typescripts as a way for me to acquire a saleable skill.

My disinclination to be distracted by a job when I left school brought a reasonable threat of being chucked out; so I got a job and carried on writing as best as I could, resentfully.

I thought my pay ridiculously low; they were pleasantly surprised; I paid my way; and pressure came to an end.

I met a Scots musician called Joe Manning, and that led to poetry and music evenings in a pub in central London, late '60s. On the way home the Metropolitan Police often liked to ask me what I had in my bag; and pushed me around when I said "Poetry books". That went on for a few years, the gigs and the police. I chucked my job; and, separately, Joe went to Australia. For myself, I had decided I couldn't handle not being a full time poet. That was 1972.

By then, I had a first idea of some things I would like to investigate in Poetry, rather than just imitating others or recording my emotions.

I spent a couple of years just being a poet and trying to make a living from it but felt too much pressure to be an entertainer; so I went back to work for a couple of years; and then I became a mature full-time student a little after the mass resignation from The Poetry Society Council.

Let me tell it another way

I acknowledged myself a poet in 1963. From then on, I was trying to find Poetry other than what was being presented to me as contemporary poetry, which alienated me.

As I walked in on my first visit to The Poetry Society, a woman handed me a glass of white wine asking, "Are you a bard?" I went there to workshops for a while; but they were not what I needed.

I went to Better Books now and then, without knowing who was who or making much contact. I watched and listened.

Once or twice I saw Bob Cobbing perform.

I attended a group in Mitcham; but not for long. Wherever I went, it was somewhat as if I wanted to note "No trace of V".

The Bec Poets met in a flat at Tooting Bec. It was no worse than anything else; and much better organised. The assumptions seemed a bit less oppressive to me than the Church of Rome's.

I suggested to the organiser that a poet I had met needed encouragement. He said that he did not want to encourage people to be poets because there was too much bad poetry already.

I'm not sure who spoke to whom first or what the circumstances were; but by the start of the '70s I was well-acquainted with Bob Cobbing, working often with him administratively and getting involved in Poets Conference, ALP etc. He was doing more than moaning or obeying idiots. Encouraged by him, I went to events at The Poetry Society.

I went to Writers Forum workshop there. It met every week. I got so much information on what Poetry could be it's a wonder I didn't turn to dust.

I met Clive Fencott, cris cheek, Jeremy Adler, Bill Griffiths, and many others, including Alaric Sumner (1952-2000), founder of *words worth* magazine, poet, painter, playwright of whose work I published a large retrospective review in *Masthead* 8 for editor Alison Croggon in 2004.

By 1974, I was on the Council Executive.

I was around the Printshop but far from the most important person there. I led the construction of and staffed the Bookshop.

From my perspective in 2014, apart from my association with Cobbing, by far the most important thing about that period for me was meeting the poet / composer Sten Hanson and others in 1972 at a Poetry Society concert conjured by Cobbing from ICES72 (*International Carnival of Experimental Sound*, centred on the Round House) + the invitation (for which I believe I should partly thank Henri Chopin) to work at Fylkingen as guest composer which was renewed several times + the other relationships I formed especially perhaps with cheek and Fencott.

They were the ones with whom I co-founded the group *jgjgjg* in 1976. I formed a lasting friendship with Alaric Sumner; and that, by swerve of shore and bend of bay, nearly thirty years on, led to collaboration with composer John Levack Drever now entering its eleventh year. And that, perhaps, has led to collaborations with composers Benedict Taylor and Tina Krekels in the second decade of this century.

By the time ACGB split our vote at the Society, I had had enough of the infighting and tantrums; and what, in a slightly different context, someone recently called embarrassment and fudging.

Robert Sheppard says that we walked out to "ineffective boycotts against the Society and – less positively – instigated acts of recrimination".[2] Not I! except perhaps, later, there was a brief desire to respond to Sheppard's accusations. (As Basil Fawlty said, "Manuel, let me explain!")

They thought about tactics. That's why they thought as they did. They discouraged creativity, replacing it with all manner of things, such as Malarkey and Mediocrity.

I remember, soon after the lost vote and resignation, coming to the conclusion that the most important thing to do, for any of us, was to make new work. Those who don't make new work will contentedly waste lifetimes quibbling.

After *jgjgjg* (i.e. after 1978), there was *Bang Crash Wallop, John & Mary Outchan, Beak, Asian Ladies* and more. Much of that saw some light of day from *Typical Characteristics* (published by Balsam Flex run by Erik Vonna-Michell), the output of which, soon to be republished, was described by Julian Cowley in *The Wire* as "writers, working with the material aspects of language, typographic shape and texture or their performed equivalent in sound."

I wouldn't stress <u>writers</u> quite as strongly. I'm quite happy with the liminal as a working environment. Performances occurred at the Film-makers Coop, Acme Gallery, London Musicians Collective and elsewhere.

From 1977, I studied, formally, English Language and Literature, History, Education then Computer Science, for over 10 years. I went irregularly to SubVoicive Poetry and other events. From 1981, I taught school and went home to partner, step-children and cat.

I dismissed the Poetry Society years as wasted; and got on with new art.

In 1991, my home relationship breaking, I went back to Writers Forum workshop and have been there ever since.

In 1994, I took over Sub-Voicive Poetry which continued for nearly 200 meetings before I suspended it in 2004.

Robert Sheppard's invitation to perform with Bob at the 'Smallest Poetry Festival in the World' (3 December 1994, at Sheppard's house in Tooting) instigated *Domestic Ambient Noise*, 300 or more booklets of it, *Collaborations* for Peter Finch and, I think, 9 other books.

In 1998, we published our co-edited *Word Score Utterance Choreography* in verbal and visual poetry. That was WF750. WF1000 was the serial publication we started to co-edit, *On Word*, which I did not continue beyond #2, once Bob had died.

In 2002, at Bob's deathbed invitation, I took on the role of co-convenor of Writers Forum, a decision he had considered for 2 years.

Let me tell it another way

The Poetry Society years were not wasted. I suspected from soon after I took office that we would lose; we were subjected to constructive dismissal. Yet I persisted and gave a lot of my time.

Had the fight been better fought; had we been more organised and united; and had those we were fighting not been quite such destructive buffoons; had their investigations been in good faith; we might have had a greater long term effect.

However... though Poetry may be written down in books, it is vital in performance, as a time-based art.

And yet I still see making of poetry to be a lot to do with revision even as I regard it as often involving improvisation collaboration.

We did a lot during those years – performances and other events, and creative cross-pollination. Perhaps not blissful, but it was good to be alive there in those years, in between the struggles. Not least when Ed Dorn read.

Those who criticised us for giving up seemed selfish; and now they seem unrealistic and maybe missing the point. We were never going to be allowed to do what we tried to do. At best, we could individually accede to absorption. Resignation to the Body Snatchers.

But, creatively, I am grateful for what happened. There isn't space to go into it here, but what I see as processes of fairly constant renewal in myself as an artist may have started then and seem to be with me now: what might seem like turbulence but is in fact a degree of constant revision I learned then, applied not just to individual works, but also to the very acts of making themselves.

NOTES

[1] Commander Powell, in *Dark Star*. Dir. John Carpenter, 1974.

[2] Robert Sheppard, *When Bad Times Made for Good Poetry* (Shearsman Books, 2011), p.17.

Tangled up in Politics

Elaine Randell

Raised in Lee Green on my mother's racy reading material of the 1950s, Stan Barstow, Alan Sillitoe and, covertly, *Lady Chatterley's Lover*, and energised by Bob Dylan lyrics and every Jack Kerouac, Gary Snyder book or anything by the Beat poets that I could get my hands on, I started up *Amazing Grace* magazine from the back bedroom of my parent's home at Horn Park Lane in 1968. I was a paid-up member of the CND and the Peace Pledge Union. My father had fought in Burma as a member of the forgotten fourteenth army, and his pacifist views of the 1950s and 1960s influenced me.

After school I would rush to Drury Lane to the Arts Lab (run by Jim Haynes) to catch up with the very cool events including Yoko Ono and John Lennon's first joint artwork 'Build Around' which was premiered there in May 1968. Sitting on the stairs of the Arts Lab, with Lennon in his white suit and beard with coffee in hand, the happy couple had come fresh from Indica, the Bloomsbury bookshop, hand in hand. The young Elaine Randell, over-eager to catch a glimpse of Lennon, hurtled down the stairs knocking the coffee over and splashing his white-suited lap. My memoir of my relationship with the Beatles, regrettably, ends there. I was 17 years old and convinced that I had a responsibility to join art and poetry together. *Amazing Grace* ran for 6 editions; the results are cringingly embarrassing and would be more so without the generous contributions of poets I had read and written to who responded warmly; including Jeff Nuttall, Mike Horovitz, Miles Gibson, James Kirkup, Martin Booth, and Barry MacSweeney. At that time, many poets corresponded regularly with one another; the poet, Jeremy Reed, from his home in the Channel Islands, wrote to me several times each week. The magazine format was laid out on my bedroom floor on huge cards stuck with cow-gum. I also had a tiny Adana press which finally defeated me; instead I took the artwork to the basement of the King's Cross bookshop, Housmans, where I had frequently lingered in my Peace Pledge Union pursuits. There, a master printer, John, sweated hard as he worked tirelessly printing left-wing pamphlets and books – and, now, copies of *Amazing Grace*

– in the basement. The copies of *Amazing Grace* were hoiked around London and sold on a sale-or-return basis. Printing costs had to be met. Subscriptions were £1 for four posted copies. At that time, small presses survived with the assured purchase of at least one copy to the British Library, several to Compendium Books, Bernard Stone at Turret and Better Books and many to American university libraries. Small press poetry was thriving, largely poorly-produced but with brilliant content. The final edition of *Amazing Grace* was in 1974. A review by *Second Aeon* says; "*Amazing Grace (5) 13p. elaine randell. a well printed mag of poetry & graphics and somehow you can tell that it's edited by a woman. uneven in content but with quite a few high spots. one of the better littles. incl: horovitz/ alan ireland/ tom pickard/ jeff nuttall (v.good)/ macsweeney/ tony rudolf's translations/ small mag reviews.*"[1] The comment, indicates how women were seen by some within the small-press world of poetry at that time. In the 1960s and early 1970s, the involvement of and work by women was relegated to second place by some – but by no means by all. A cursory glimpse at the number of men whose work was published by UK small presses against the number of women reveals much. In the USA, women poets like Joanna Kyger, Faye Kicknosway and Anne Waldmann were also finding it hard to make their mark.

My first real job was with Marshall's Silver Antiques in Chancery Lane. Mr Sylvester, the owner of the shop, was no stranger to the literary world and was happy to take me on when I told him that I was a poet. His daughter, the actress Jacqueline Sylvester, was married to Frank Marcus who had written *The Killing of Sister George* in 1964, a landmark play about a female nurse who, it was implied, was a lesbian, an almost taboo topic at the time. I was later offered a job working in the Rare and Antiquarian book department at Foyle's in Charing Cross Road, opposite Better Books, and my colleague and friend, Reg Read, and I welcomed in first editions of poetry and ephemera, usually sending them to the USA. First editions of new work – *Man Does Women Is, Crow* etc – were also collected. However, I shunned the mainstream poetry of the time, finding no resonance between their world and mine. But, to be fair, I did not even try; to me it was *just old*. In my spare time I typed letters for *International Times* magazine at the home of its co-editor, David Mairovitz. These were often about the Vietnam war; letters to General Westmoreland, named by Mairovitz in

International Times as "General Wastemoreland". These were heady, and in hindsight, important times. A glimpse at the archives, now on line, of IT shows the numerous poetry events held in London in addition to tiny adverts for gigs by bands such as The Doors, Pink Floyd, Traffic. IT was known for being a literary and artistic avant-garde magazine with a large contingent of the editorial board from Oxbridge.[2] This was the heart of the Hippie Underground movement, influenced heavily by the Beat poets and music. I recall seeing William Burroughs at the Phun City festival in 1970, which was run by Mick Farren with his underground community bands, the Pretty Things, Pink Fairies and the Edgar Broughton Band.

My next job as a rare-book cataloguer and general factotum was at the Covent Garden Bookshop, Long Acre. This brought me into contact with the brilliant poet and my great friend, Tony Rudolf, who was involved in the publication of Barry MacSweeney's book *Brother Wolf* by Bernard Stone at Turret Books.[3] Barry and I married in 1972. My own career had returned, at that stage, to my original training as an art therapist in a psychiatric hospital in North Kent. Ideas about anti-psychiatry, including those of R. D. Laing and Timothy Leary, abounded at the time, but did not reflect the needs of the patients I met then, who were frequently older people suffering trauma from the Second World War or depressed women addicted to Valium. My career took a turn again into media when I became deputy editor of one of the first give-away magazines in London, *Sophisticat*, based in Pimlico. The three-day week of 1974 brought challenges, with no electricity after 10pm.[4] Barry had been working for the National Maritime Museum in Greenwich as a picture restorer in the early 1970s but had retained his passion and clear skill as a journalist in everything he did. *Sophisticat* needed a book reviewer, and Barry fitted the bill. This encouraged him to return to mainstream journalism, which he did at the *Folkestone and Hythe Gazette and Herald*. Ted Heath was the local MP. Barry's involvement and strength of feeling for the miners' strike and his work with the NUJ at that time was a very major part of his life. Barry felt passionately about the oppression of the working man throughout his life. Firm friendship at that time with Allen and Elaine Fisher is recalled with great fondness. We were invited to join the Poetry Society's Committee and along with Lee Harwood, Allen Fisher, Roger Guedalla, Bob Cobbing,

Lawrence Upton, Kit Wright, John Cotton and Laurence Cotterell, we entered the lion's den of other people's agendas. I was the only woman. It's hard to recall events of the Poetry Society without thinking of the White House Pub next door. The poet and alcoholic, Eddie Linden, was a feature of every post-Council meeting in the White House. I read now of Eddie's tragic childhood that he never revealed at the time.[5] His friend, the poet John Heath-Stubbs, was also a constant figure. The calm, steady figure of Ian Robinson, Peter Hodgkiss and indeed a long-suffering Poetry Society clerk, Barbara, should also not be forgotten for their helpful moderating influence and support. There were also interesting American figures around the White House pub at the time, allegedly from the CIA, interested in knowing more about *these poets* and their underground small presses. Perhaps the name of the pub was a draw for them.

What struck me at the time, and remains with me now, is how badly usually reasonable and rational people behaved towards one another over poetry. But of course it wasn't about poetry; it was about power, control, class and money. The battle brought out and revealed the worst and the best in several individuals. Many have written eloquently about the *"real issues"* and their assumptions about them at that time. There was much occupying of moral high ground and, when this was coupled with a total lack of flexibility and a desire to win, the conflict ended badly but, in my view, predictably. I was one of the few Council members who did not leave when others left. Lee Harwood and Roy Fisher also remained. Barry had been the Chairman during these difficult times, and he wrote at the time, *"I've done too much compromising and my skull won't take any more."* For my part, I do not recall too much compromise, but chairing in such an emotionally charged climate was a super-human task. I stated then, and I believe it now, that there was a middle ground to be had and compromise was possible. Sadly, the chaos made many appear brutal and others reactionary. While there is no victory in war, what was important was an injection of life into an unwilling and a non-consenting patient, the moribund and narrow-minded establishment that the Poetry Society had become. Under the editorship of Eric Mottram, *Poetry Review*, which had been seen as a conservative magazine, introduced the new, young innovative breathing poets. We were pleased to be breaking into that establishment magazine at last. I read that the Poetry Society still has its rucks – with Chairmen resigning and tempers rising – it must be something about the written word and Arts Council loot.

While the Poetry Society work took effort and time, Barry and I had been running the Black Suede Boot Press, publishing Nicholas Moore's book, *Spleen*, Jeremy Prynne's *Fire Lizard*, and Barry's book *Fool's Gold*. Nicholas Moore would write to us several times a day, letters with poems and phrases that covered every yellow envelope. Nicholas's wife was a schizophrenic, and our visits to their home were always more than memorable. Nicholas spoke of his parents, the philosophers George Moore and Dorothy Ely, and also of his friend, the poet David Gascoyne, who we hoped would allow us to publish his poems. We met David when he was still highly vulnerable but much supported by his new wife, Judy Lewis, whom he had recently married. Later, as Secret Books, I went on to publish Tom Raworth, Allen Fisher, Tony Lopez and Paul Matthews.

Barry and I were invited by his friend Fred Buck to stay in his home near Boston, USA. We also spent time with Fred's mother Helene, who made exquisite found glass sculptures. Fred was a family man, proud of his two daughters; he worked as a postman. His own extraordinary childhood had shown him the importance of stability. We then stayed with Joel Oppenheimer and Allen Ginsberg in New York. Joel was working for the *Village Voice* at that time; he was a recovering alcoholic with a passion for baseball, words and poetry, possibly in that order.[6] At an overcrowded party of about 80 people in two rooms at Allen's, Bob Dylan and Roger McGuinn arrived, which, on reflection, will have accounted for the crush. The 1970s were coming to a close.

I was to return to the USA in 1980. Allen Ginsberg had invited me to his home in Boulder, and I was to read at Naropa. Allen was away at the time, but a vivid recollection of my stay was the sight of a small roll of bedding on the floor of a chaotic, small bedroom. This belonged to Billy Burroughs, son of William. Father and son had recently reunited; sadly Billy was to die a few months later. Eric Mottram had encouraged me to contact poets in Bolinas, and at Joanne Kyger's beach-front home she hosted an evening where she spoke, with some passion, about the women poets who had successfully supported the lives of their more prominently published male partners in addition to writing themselves, some also while raising children: Bobbie Louise Hawkins, Alice Notley, Hettie Jones to name but a few. Barry and I had relatively recently separated, and speaking about co-existing with complex men was on my agenda.

What cannot be overstated, when recalling these times in both the UK and the USA, was the influence and support of Eric Mottram and his capacity to communicate and connect. His energetic dinner parties at Herne Hill with piles of books lining the stairs, were renowned; he provided fabulous meals and gave impromptu generous non-stop lectures on extraordinarily fascinating topics. Eric was driven by many things; he thought in time-lines, about influences, about context, seemingly without effort. I recall him speaking on the connection between the lock and the gun, throwing in a further connection with Bartók's early works along with a history of American poetry and art to the present day. Eric was generous; he lived to the full; and his legacy, for many, was his untiring dedication in helping others to reach their potential, particularly as artists and poets. While he did not suffer fools, he also had the grace not to highlight others' clearly unequal intellect.

Notes

[1] *Second Aeon* 15, p. 151. *Second Aeon* (1966-74) was edited by Peter Finch.

[2] *International Times* was set up by Jim Haynes, Jack Henry Moore, Michael Henshaw, John Hopkins, Sue Miles and Barry Miles. The dramatist Tom McGrath, who had edited *Peace News*, was editor; David Mairowitz was assistant editor. Indica Books provided its basement as an office.

[3] For an account of the activities of Tony Rudolf's own press in this period, see Tony Rudolf, *Menard Press, 1969-2009* (Menard Press, 2010). Menard Press was particularly important for its publication of poetry in translation.

[4] In response to the successful miners' strike, Ted Heath's Conservative government introduced a three-day working week to conserve electricity. This austerity measure came into force in January 1974 and provided the context for the general election in February.

[5] Eddie Linden was a poet and editor of the magazine *Aquarius* (1969-93). Sebastian Barker published a biography, *Who Is Eddie Linden?*, in 1979.

[6] Joel Oppenheimer (1930-88) was a New York poet and former student at Black Mountain College. He was the first director of the St Mark's Poetry Project (1966-68) and wrote a column for *Village Voice* from 1969 to 1984.

Working with Bob Cobbing through the 1970s

Paula Claire

On returning to England in 1968 after 4 years' TEFL in Athens, I had published my *Mobile Poems Greece*,[1] participatory texts with non-linear clusters inviting improvisation, and had high hopes of finding people who could perform them with me, but even young actors were fazed. Clues appeared: at Better Books I'd discovered the international *Anthology of Concrete Poetry*[2] containing a British contingent including Bob Cobbing; caught him reading his *ABC in Sound*[3] on the BBC Third Programme; then joining the Poetry Society I grabbed the opportunity to hear him live at their Conference, September 1969. What an ear-and-eye-opener! Bob splattered, bombarded, engulfed us with his untrammelled voice, exposed us to his text-scores, all the letters of words strewn over the page – *Whississippi* – my favourite, a duo he'd just recorded for Fylkingen in Sweden.[4] In my chapter in *The Salt Companion to Bill Griffiths*[5] I describe in detail my conversation with Bob that dinnertime – how he improvised my poem 'Mykonos in Sunlight'[6] with me as I'd dreamed it could should sound.

The day after Boxing Day I was invited to Bob and Jennifer's abode. Laden shelves bowed with books. Mind out! Stalagmites of books. Up one corner a double bed spread with fabric, Bob's favourite blacksgreys merging into an ancient longhaired tabby mog curled up asleep half-hidden among scattered papers. Bob picked up a handful. "Let's give these a whirl." Hastily putting down my own bag of poems... somewhere ... unmuffling myself from my wintercoathatscarfgloves... dumping them... somewhere, I grasped what he proffered. A spray of typewritten letters when cohered saying "a voluble cascade of rippling water emancipates the light."[7] Away we went on flurries of sound: the cat's ears twitched not: immune.

My tattered copy of *kurrirrurriri*,[8] a collection of sound poems he then gave me, became my bible for our performances during 1970 (the first major one at St Martin's School of Art) along with *&etc*,[9] another motley collection, including permutated words, some based on female names, in particular 'Gail song'. These showed exceptional ingenuity in their rigorous mathematical patterning. I analysed several using colour flow-pens to reveal this, having trained in analysing modern musical structures – my teacher had learnt from Humphrey Searle, a pupil of Webern. This booklet signed "Paula Claire March '70" indicates my new-found status as a confirmed poet, family maiden name gone.

1970 was a total immersion in all facets of Bob's indefatigable dedication to exploring new forms, compelling us to re-evaluate our ideas of what poetry comprehends: visually challenging prints perceived as exciters of vocal performance, a synaesthetic approach I revel in. I was inspired by his multifarious techniques executed through his mimeograph machine: typewriter visuals treated with over-printings; exploration of textures achieved by ink splurging; crumpling the stencil before employing it; the dance of pressed-on letters; collage and verbal found material.[10] Every time we met – my appointment diaries indicate a fortnightly pattern of Tuesdays for a run-through of current works – we would visit his long-suffering Gestetner in its little room ankle-deep in its evacuations, for Bob to pounce on a cluster for us to work on. Often he overtaxed it and it conked out causing him great anxiety: "I implore the technician not to fix it *too* much." Bob embraced happy accidents, avowing "Every accident is a new departure." Then we would repair to the Poetry Society, 21 Earls Court Square, to share our vocal explorations in his workshop, a magnet for like-minded poets and enthusiasts, not only British but from all over the world.

BOUNDLESS POETRY

Regarding our re-hear-sallies, he was obviously pleased that my young female voice created a valuable contrast to his male growl, and that I was not intimidated by his huge outbursts of vocal inventiveness, thanks to my singing in a choir from a young age and an innate love of improvisation nurtured by going to concerts of jazz and Indian music. To his credit we worked on my pieces as much as his which made them come on in leaps and bounds – literally. By April I'd created *DANCE*, using fragmented rhythmic language patterns, so we met Ballet Rambert director Norman Maurice hoping to convince him. NO. Dancers to speak while dancing to our sound poetry score? Impossible – wouldn't have enough puff!

I savour a Workshop that summer when Jeremy Adler spied a good number of large empty cardboard boxes in the hallway, left over from a delivery of new chairs[11]. "Each of you get in one and make your own sounds," he commanded. A delightful cacophony arose, reminding me of London Zoo dawn chorus – I once lived opposite. "I'll never see him again," I muttered – I'd invited my new boyfriend, stained-glass artist Paul San Casciani – "must think me bonkers." Then I heard him emitting peculiar clicking noises, a cross between champagne corks and the mating calls of a capercaillie. That moment cemented us for life: engaged shortly afterwards.

At the Poetry Society, along with a nub of supporters, Bob was the dynamo of change on the General Council. He roped me into being Treasurer and Membership Secretary of his new initiative, Poets Conference: we held our first meetings there in June, the express aims being payment for poets' readings and more poetry for more people. October 1970 he amalgamated ideas from the Conference and produced a Document setting out ambitious plans for a bookshop, liquid/solid refreshments, library, print room and recording studio, rebranded the National Poetry Centre. Alongside all this I was exposed to the diversity of innovative poets he published in Writers Forum and gave me. In those early days I was particularly fascinated by the typewriter poems of Dom Sylvester Houédard, who created virtuoso "typestracts", symbolic images expressing philosophical ideas from Far Eastern religions, exemplified in *Tantric poems perhaps* (WF) and ...*like contemplation...* (WF 83, February 1972) and Jiri Valoch's *Nine Optical Poems*[21] (WF 36, November 1967), typed over-printings displaying striking optical effects, a big influence on my typewriter "text-iles" I developed over the next 30 years.

1970 came to a climax with Bob inviting me, accompanied by my fiancé, to exhibit and perform in the seminal *?concrete poetry* exhibition, Stedelijk Museum Amsterdam in November that he had helped to arrange, contributing the 'Sound Poetry' essay to the Catalogue. There I met many practitioners including Eugen Gomringer and Hansjörg Mayer who opened the show by playing "ping-pong" – a concrete text of Gomringer's – attuning our ears to the delicate patterns of sound as the ball was struck back and forth.[12] Bob's publication for our performance was *sOnicicOns* (WF 63, November 1970). We regaled them with

SUEsequence an intriguing sound poem made from the fragmented sounds in 'Kleenex Boutique Tissues', subsequently a wow in our recording for Dial-a-Poem; its visual form stuck-on letters careering and swooping ending in a scherzo.[13] A contrast was the sonorous *Hymn to the Sacred Mushroom* (WF), comprising ancient vocabulary Bob had researched, a homage to the shamanic traditions of Mongolian culture, which became his "signature tune" – we performed that over the years more than any other piece, eliciting from Bob his deepest foghorn. Taking part in this event gave me an international perspective I have never lost, helped by another rare female exhibitor (exhibition ratio: 137 men; 7 women – typical of the formidable gender-bias of the 1970s), the poet and art critic Mirella Bentivoglio, contacting me with an invitation to the shows she curated to promote female experimental poets whose existence she zealously researched and with whom I have exchanged work ever since.

I was initially published by Writers Forum in the first *Kroklok*, a magazine of historical and contemporary sound poetry edited by Dom Sylvester Houédard, which we launched at the ICA in February 1971. It included my typewriter shaped poems 'Breeze' and 'Energygalaxy'. Bob gave me his "mock-up" to work with, and I annotated the pieces we presented: the historical ones on 17 February with Dom Sylvester; a range of our own work the following week, filmed by Westphalian TV, who completed their project when we participated in the International Sound Poetry Festival at Wilhemsbad-by-Hanau that May, a month after my marriage. Bob's production of the 'p and l poem' intrigued by the engagement ring Paul designed for me with the legend "PA UL AN DP AU LA" is dated 1/60 21.2.71. It became the middle poem of *Three Poems for Voice and Movement* (WF 70, March 1971), which we presented at his workshop. In June Bob founded Konkrete Canticle to record work on an Arts Council LP.[14] This was to be launched at the opening of the first phase of the Amsterdam exhibition in the three showings in the UK: Walker Art Gallery Liverpool, October 1971, then MOMA Oxford Feb 1972 – we did not risk Belfast. We were the first sound-poetry performance group in Great Britain, parallel to The Four Horsemen in Toronto, founded in the same period.[15]

A highlight of our work together was letting fly to a packed Southwark Cathedral of Bob's concrete poem *15 Shakespeare Kaku* on 23 April 1972. This was published, with other poets' work written specially for the occasion, as *Poems for Shakespeare* by the Globe Playhouse Trust. Using fragments, overlays and distortions of the title intensified these compact images, producing from Bob and me, backed up by staggering blasts from Michael Chant on the cathedral organ, a gamut of sounds emblematic of Shakespeare's plays' many moods. My mock-up performance score, annotated according to our rehearsals, I made into a quickly-flipped concertina-fold. Bob later published *15 Shakespeare Kaku* in a delightful small format volume (WF 86, October 1972) price 2½p. (!). In May he published my set of eight typewriter visual poems *Soundsword* (WF 85), and we presented these with my characteristic audience participation at the NPC. It was around this time I remember a bloke walking into Bob's workshop in dark gear and chains. Sat down next to me. I blinked. His hands pinged out "love": "hate". Had he come to do us over? He read quietly an extraordinary poem. Bill Griffiths.

From 1972 onwards I became increasingly influenced by Cobbing's pieces such as *The Judith Poem* (WF 81, November 1971) and *Mary Rudolph's Chromosomes* (WF 87, October 1972), in which distortions of letterforms, smudges and blobs predominated that we interpreted in sound; and observing my baby's fingers brailling the textures on whatever I was wearing I became convinced that our languages have evolved though hypersensitivity to markings. First exploration of my "gestation of language" research aiming to dredge ancestral responses deep in the subconscious was at Bob's workshop, May 1973, thanks to Jeremy Adler and Bill Griffiths being game to join me in vocal improvisation to the text-ures of a variety of actual stones, pebbles, flints, pumice, I'd garnered from various locations – Bob had initially doubted it could happen. Later I had them photographed and made collages of these, published as *Stone Tones* (WF 112) in August 1974. Concrete poetry was now my natural medium and I embarked on a series of scorch-mark poems attempting to get to grips with phenomenal energies – magmatic, solar, nuclear – and the horror of weapons proliferation that haunted us at that period. The first was *Magma* (WF 106), which was included in *Pen as Pencil: Drawings and Paintings by British Authors*, arranged by the National Book League for Europalia 73 in Belgium and infiltrated by some visual poets including Bob and me. 'FissionFusion' was printed in *WF 100* and performed at the mighty celebratory get-together at the NPC.

The greater open-mindedness to poetic forms Bob's range of workshops fostered is evident in the exponential increase in the variety of poetry appearing in the Society's magazine, *Poetry Review*. Articles and selections of visual poetry by Peter Mayer for *Poetry Review* 61.3 (Autumn 1970) included my first official publication, 'Chartres Windows: Winter'. Major developments took place under Eric Mottram's enterprising editorship, Autumn 1971 till Summer 1977: his great knowledge of cutting-edge literature here and in the USA demonstrated in his choice; most covers featured visual poetry, even my photomicrograph tracing performance score 'Cucumber Wilt x 500' (Winter 1974).

Bob and I took an epic day-return to Sunderland for *Bob Cobbing & Writers Forum*, a major retrospective put on by Ceolfrith Arts Centre, and the subject of Ceolfrith Press Number 26 October 1974: articles, exhibition list and an invaluable Writers Forum checklist, the most comprehensive survey of Bob's work at that time. In the afternoon I gave an interactive programme of my own work, showing its relationship with Writers Forum, then joined Bob for a warmly-received performance of his poems in the evening.

As a founder member of the annual International Sound Poetry Festival in Sweden, Bob valiantly organised the next four Festivals at the NPC, its main room newly kitted out with stage lighting. The seventh was a wide-ranging programme, 2-9 June 1974, of readings, discussions and an exhibition where I showed *Moon Omen*, a stained glass appliqué panel in collaboration with my husband. Sean O'Huigin published his impressions of the Eighth Festival, 14-23 May 1975, in *Open Letter* 3 including his snapshot of me performing 'Poetry Laurels', handing round variegated laurel leaves for all to respond vocally to their unique markings. There I met bpNichol, a wonderfully expansive performer and great organiser of the Canadian scene. The programme also featured the accomplished and distinctive performance of Danish poet Lily Greenham.[16]

By the time of the Ninth Festival at the NPC Bob had published *Codesigns* (WF 135, April 1976), my tracings of photomicrographs. My theme for the Festival was inspired by my visit to Iran, invited by the family of my Zoroastrian student in Oxford whose brother taught at Pahlavi University, Shiraz, where I gave a lecture-performance on International Concrete Poetry.[61] My Festival performance concluded with pouring oil onto buckets of water, calling everyone to improvise vocally with Farsi words to their iridescent swirls. At the Tenth Festival, May 1977, I shared an evening with Lily Greenham, my programme poems in English/Arabic from my trip to Saudi Arabia, and Bob's latest publications for me, *Antibody Quipu* (WF 163, May 1977,) which comprised the code of an antibody cut into strips I hung from the door lintel compelling everyone to negotiate their way through this "fly curtain", and ending with *Sign If I Can Ces* (WF 148, December 1976), tracings of woodknots: everyone falling to their knees and sounding the wood-knots on the floorboards.

After the Great Rumpus of the meeting convened by the Arts Council in July 1977, when all those committed to an inclusive and progressive attitude to poetry resigned from the Society, including myself, Bob, undeterred, transferred his events – and us – to the London Musicians Collective, 42 Gloucester Avenue, NW1, a tatty old railway building but providing a large performance space with a pub conveniently opposite for all necessities.

In 1977 Bob was invited to the Berlin Festival's DADA theme and consequent focus on sound poetry, seizing this opportunity to re-form Konkrete Canticle with Bill Griffiths replacing Michael Chant, our debut Berlin. Our combined idiosyncratic talents offered a great variety of approaches to innovative poetry that led to major performances during 1977-79 as detailed in *The Salt Companion to Bill Griffiths*. Our trip to Toronto to perform at the 11th International Sound Poetry Festival gave us the incentive to create works specifically for our group.[17] Attracted to the latest advert for Gordon's gin, a bold section of its calligraphic name, I incorporated this in a cut-up hand poem on a string, *Gingle* (WF 221, September 1978) – we whirled many over the audience. Bob then adopted the image in *Ginetics* (WF 220, August 1978). Bill contributed Gin vocabulary for our collaborative chapbook *Gin Chap* (WF 227, December 1978). We all visited the Niagara Falls, the Canadian Horseshoe side, and responded with *NiagarA* (WF 225, December 1978), 'NiagarB' (published as *The Horseshoe Falls*, WF 232, February 1979) and my *NiagarC* (WF 235, April, 1979) – first performance in Munster. We also each visited a range of different Ontario schools, paired with a Canadian poet. Bob published my *Silver Birch Morse* (WF 237, April 1979), dedicated to my visit to Manitoulin Island School where we all improvised to birch bark unwound from the tree-trunks. In December he marked my English/Italian performance in the Venice Biennale at Mirella Bentivoglio's show *Materialisation of Language* by publishing my *Codestones of Venice* (WF 229, December 1978).[18] By this time I had collected so much material I began to write my *Archive Catalogue One*, finishing it for publication at the official opening by Mirella Bentivoglio in May 1980.[19]

Bob was gratified that he and Writers Forum received recognition in *The Open and Closed Book – Contemporary Book Art*, a major exhibition at the Victoria & Albert Museum London, 12 September – 18 November 1979, that included a Concrete Poetry Section illustrated with over 30 practitioners including my *Meiosis* (WF 197, April 1978), a concertina-fold of my tracings of stages of cell division, a score for performance. Bob's unquenchable urge to explore the full expression of poetry ever sustains me. Opposite the contents page of my Golden Anniversary book, 2012, I wrote: "Thanks Bob for your unflinching and unswerving example."[20]

Notes

[1] *Mobile Poems Greece* (Oxford, 1968).

[2] Emmett Williams (ed), *Anthology of Concrete Poetry* (NY: Something Else Press / Stuttgart: Edition Hansjörg Mayer, 1967).

[3] *ABC in Sound*, WF 12 (January 1965).

[4] *Whississippi* ,WF 47 (July 1969). Premiere at April 1969 *Text-Composition Festival*, Stockholm, run by Fylkingen, a group committed to all aspects of modern music, founded 1933, who initiated the annual Text-Sound Composition Festivals.

[5] 'Bill Griffiths: A Severe Case of Hypergraphia', in Will Rowe (ed), *The Salt Companion to Bill Griffiths* (Cambridge: Salt, 2007), pp. 37-50.

[6] Included in *Mobile Poems Greece*.

[7] 'Cascade' (1969); published in *Ceolfrith* 26, 1974.

[8] *Kurrirrurriri* , WF 37 (October 1969).

[9] *&etc* (Cardiff: Vertigo Press, 1970).

[10] See Bob Cobbing, *Changing Forms in English Visual Poetry – the Influence of Tools and Machines*, WF (December 1988) for a detailed account.

[11] Jeremy Adler, concrete poet, later Professor of German at King's College, London.

[12] Eugen Gomringer, 'ping pong', *Anthology of Concrete Poetry*; for a fuller account of this event, see my essay 'See Jig Saw –an essay in/on concrete poetry'.

[13] *SUEsequence*, Private Edition (14 August 1970); Dial-a-Poem, Tuesday 12 January 1971.

[14] Konkrete Canticle: Bob Cobbing, Paula Claire, Michael Chant. Chant left to concentrate on the Scratch Orchestra c.1973, Side One of the LP was 'Experiments in Disintegrating Language'; Side Two was 'Konkrete Canticle'.

[15] The Four Horsemen was a Canadian Performance Poetry Group: bpNichol, Paul Dutton, Steve McCaffery, and Rafael Barreto-Rivera..

[16] Lily Greenham (1924-2001) was an active member of the *Wiener Gruppe*, engaged in experimental theatre works in Vienna during the 1950s. During the 1960s, she worked in Paris as a visual artist as part of the *Groupe de Recherche d'Art Visuel*. She moved to London in 1972 and worked on "lingual music", text-based compositions using electronics and multi-tracking. She worked with the BBC Radiophonic Workshop and was part of the LMC network.

[17] Held at the St Lawrence Centre, Toronto. See Steve McCaffery and bpNichol (eds), *Sound Poetry: A Catalogue* (Toronto: Underwhich Editions, 1978).

[18] *Materializzazione del Linguaggio*, Old Salt Store, Venice, 20 September – 15 October 1978.

[19] *International Concrete Poetry Archive Catalogue One* (Oxford: ICPA, 1980).

[20] *Going for Gold Part One: My Life in Poetry – 50 Years Sustained* (Oxford: ICPA, 2012).

Whispers from the past

VALERIE SOAR

i.m. Bill Griffiths, Eric Mottram, Geoffrey Soar

I went to UCL in 1967 where Geoffrey was the English & Special Collections Librarian. When we met, I was 18, he was 36. Geoffrey had wanted to read Architecture at Cambridge, but his scholarship had taken him to St John's to read English, where he was much influenced by F. R. Leavis and Hugh Sykes Davies. This was in the early 1950s. Drawing, painting and etching were his passion: he took 3 years leave from UCL in the '70s to take a Fine Art degree at Byam Shaw. Languages were another passion, Italian being his favourite (he studied at the Università per Stranieri in Perugia) and in later life he studied Modern Greek. He also had a wide and deep interest in music, his favourites being Chicago and Delta Blues and the songs of Schubert.

In 1969 Geoffrey introduced me to his little-magazine and under-ground press collection, a totally alien world to me, and then started taking me to readings – another totally alien world. I soon realised that, while I might not understand much of what I was hearing, these were *really* interesting people – mostly men it has to be said. Often Jennifer Pyke Cobbing and myself were the only females in the room. I remember at a Sub-Voicive, upstairs in the Three Cups, there was an elderly poet, possibly French, who was reading, and he said with his next piece he required two females from the audience to take part, Jennifer and I just looked at each other...

Geoffrey's world at UCL was very difficult, despite someone at a poetry conference in the '70s saying that it was easy for those in rich establishments to amass little magazines. This was certainly not the case with Geoffrey's collection: every penny had to be fiercely fought for. Most of his Library "colleagues" had no feelings for this material. I remember one of them saying he wouldn't recognise a little mag if he saw one, and, if he did, he would throw it in the nearest rubbish bin. There was little support in the Department either. This stuff wasn't taught at that time, and after Steve Fender left to take up a Chair at Sussex, Geoffrey had no allies. Much of the collection was built by

Geoffrey buying things himself at readings and events.

In 1988, overtures were made via the Arts Council for an exhibition to be mounted from Geoffrey's collection (this eventually became 'little mags and how they got that way') involving the dreaded Charles Osborne.[1] Geoffrey was terribly anxious about this situation because of the Poetry Society/*Poetry Review* débacle in the '70s, and he asked me to talk to Eric Mottram about it.[2] Geoffrey was very conscious of the hurt and anger which ran so deep even a decade later. Like a lamb to the slaughter, I talked to Eric, and still vividly remember the response I got from him. Strangely, Bob Cobbing appeared to be more sanguine about this...

Geoffrey always fought for his collection, not least when it was housed in a damp basement at the back of UCL which flooded when there were heavy downpours. The underground press was literally underground – all that rare, fragile material housed in damp conditions in a place often designated as a "hard hat" area. At least while Geoffrey looked after it, the collection was, mostly, all together. Now parts are in the National Archive at Kew, parts in an underground bunker somewhere in Essex, and God knows where the rest of it is.

Geoffrey formally introduced me to Eric Mottram around 1972, although I obviously knew of him already, at some reading or other, in a bookshop/café, in Central London, possibly around Covent Garden. That was my formal introduction to the great, explosive force of nature that was Eric. I also remember going with Geoffrey to the King's Readings – there were always two poets and a table with books for sale. The audience was seldom large, and everyone, including the readers, seemed to know each other. I vividly remember watching Eric watching the audience as they were reflected in the windows. I'm not sure how many of them realised they were being scrutinised like that! Then there was a day of lectures in Senate House: Eric closed his paper with a lambasting of those poets whom he described as personal and anecdotal – "as if *anyone* would be interested in their dull little lives". He was followed by Lee Harwood, who said, very quietly, "oh dear, I fear *I am* rather personal and anecdotal".

As with a lot of the poets – Bob Cobbing, Lawrence Upton, Gavin Selerie, Harry Gilonis etc – I can't remember exactly when I first met Bill Griffiths. It would have been in the early '70s. Although an unlikely pairing, Bill and I got on right from the start, and it was a friendship which lasted until his untimely death in 2007.

In the period when I first met Bill, there were readings and events at the Film Makers' Co-operative – a brick building, the upper rooms reached by means of an outside, rickety iron staircase, in a long road, which felt like the middle of nowhere. Bill had decided to perform one of his Japanese Noh plays, handed me a "script," and I found myself cast as an angel. While this performance was in progress, behind us was Allen Fisher doing a very large painting, which I think he was working on throughout the evening.

Once Bill moved to Durham, after his houseboat burnt out, we met less often because of the distance. I did meet him in Durham when the AUT had its Winter Council at the University.[3] Bill took me round the Cathedral – it was between carol services so was lit only by candles. Being "talked" round the Cathedral, lit only by candles, by Bill Griffiths was absolute magic. After Eric died in 1995, his life, in over 500 boxes, arrived in Kidderpore Avenue to be catalogued. Bill was appointed as the archivist, and he persuaded me to come over. Once I got used to seeing the organised chaos of Guernsey Grove crowded into all those cardboard boxes, I did what I could to give Bill a hand with this massive task, spending a day a week, plus most weekends, there. We transcribed, proof-read, cross-checked, listed and shuffled things around to create some order. Bill had a keyboard over there, and, when he gave us the odd break from Eric's life and work, he'd play me some Brahms. Bill was absolutely meticulous with Eric's work, letters and papers, and we had a wonderful two years working on this stuff until the funding for Bill ran out.

Bob Cobbing seemed to have been around for as long as I can remember – partly because of his distinctive appearance and even more distinctive performances. Also, he went to Enfield Grammar School where Geoffrey's father had been the Headmaster: he had often told Geoffrey about this boy who had a deep interest in Art. Bob's chair at readings was reserved with a plastic carrier bag containing books for the book stall, and there were the days he spent manning the Writers Forum book stall at small press fairs, often taking visitors by surprise with the occasional verbal performance. One year, over in darkest Tooting when Robert Sheppard had his Smallest Poetry Festival, Bob was doing one of his vocals, by the window in the front room. He was dressed in white and had various "instruments" – I remember bells and sticks. The sun shone on him, and, as bizarre as this sounds, this rather elderly, not very tall and slightly rotund figure was transformed into something absolutely beautiful in both vision and sound. I was very privileged, on my 50th birthday in 1999, in the room above the Three Cups pub to have Bob and Lawrence perform one of their vocals while Jennifer danced (looking like a young girl as she moved). The looks of utter amazement on the faces of some of the people there, who had never, ever been to an ordinary poetry reading, let alone seen or heard anything like this, still remains with me.

Bob was always very kind to me. When he was producing *Motley for Mottram* for Eric's 70th birthday, he said to me "I want a page from you".[4] I was taken aback at this, but he persisted, and in the end, I sent my offering. I was so touched by his response, and the huge amount of care he put in on my piece, his attention to the different ways he could produce it, as if I were an established poet.

I was always at the edge of this world, but these three beautiful, outstanding men – Bill, Eric and Geoffrey shaped my life –

> so much brilliance,
>   so much talent,
> so much hope
>   now all gone.

Notes

[1] The exhibition 'little mags and how they got that way' (Co-curated with David Miller), Level 5 and Poetry Library, Royal Festival Hall, London, 1990.

[2] For a fuller account of this context, see Peter Barry, *Poetry Wars* (Cambridge: Salt Publishing, 2006).

[3] The Association of University Teachers, later the University and College Union.

[4] Bob Cobbing and Bill Griffith (eds), *Motley for Mottram* (Amra Imprint / Writers Forum, 1994). My contribution was a mesosistic using "eric mottram" as the string.

Beige Leather Trousers, Orange Dungarees

ANTHONY HOWELL

In 1969, I came back from teaching Creative Writing to American students who were spending their gap year studying at Grenoble University. This had been a time of good skiing, since Ed Resor, son of the Secretary to the US Army and one of my students, had a neat car that could get us up to the slopes while we listened to The Band as we cornered hair-pin bends. There was very good dope to be had in Grenoble, and a nice open-minded girl living in the same building as I did. She had been the girlfriend of the guy from whom I scored (and he wore beige leather trousers and had three nipples and listened to The Savage Rose). I got my own pair of beige leather trousers. The press-stud that held them together above the zip had an embarrassing habit of popping open when I sprawled on a sofa. The Savage Rose never made it in the UK, but they were big in Europe, and deservedly so. In *Rolling Stone* magazine, Lester Bangs described Anisette as "Minnie Mouse on a belladonna jag" and spoke of organ notes "pouring like star drifts from vast black skies." Anisette's is one of the great voices of the seventies. The group was Danish, but they often sang in English. The song we loved most was 'My Family was Gay' – *I don't know, I don't know, I don't know if you're my father or my brother. I don't know if you're my sister or my lover...*

I read at Poetry International in the Royal Festival Hall, and was photographed with Ginsberg – on an old-meets-young ticket. We smiled, but exchanged no words. My most vivid memory of Ginsberg is of him reading with absolute brilliance from *The Making of Americans* at an all night homage to Gertrude Stein held at Saint Mark's in the Bowery around that time. John Cage was there. There were not enough chairs, so Cage sat on Ginsberg's lap. They were like two teddy bears together.

New York figured a lot in the plans of young writers and artists in those days. We flew over to read in art galleries – Seton and Kiki Smith once organised a reading for me among sculptural blocks created by their father Tony Smith – or to get laid in the lofts of friends or get pissed in Tribeca bars. People liked to shoot pool and get into fights.

Several British artists were to move there more or less permanently in ensuing years – Anthony McCall and James Nares, among others, and my old colleague from Hornsey College of Art, the artist Robert Janz.

I suppose I was better known then than I have ever been since, and I got invited to participate in the Writers on Tour scheme organised by the Arts Council. I found myself touring Yorkshire with the likes of Melvyn Bragg, A. S. Byatt, Al Alvarez and Alan Bennett. Unfortunately, my youthful promise as a lyrical but conservative poet had been drastically subverted by my contact with the New York School. I had been invited to the Foreign Writers' Program in Iowa, a year or so before, on the strength of my versions of Imr al Kais (*Imruil* – published by Barrie & Jenkins) – and had spent vacations in New York with John Ashbery and visited Clark Coolidge in New Lebanon, and so, from the point of view of the establishment, I was hopelessly corrupted, and persisted in reading my most abstract texts to the audience gathered in Buxton or wherever we were reading that night, to the raised eyebrows of my fellow writers. Al was positively scandalised – only Alan Bennett remained consistently friendly, amusing and amused by it all in his own downbeat way.

In the late '60s I had earned a little money working for Bernard Stone at his bookshop in Kensington Church Walk. At first this was just the corner shop in a location associated with Ezra Pound, whose bronze by De Witte presided there. Then later, Bernard moved to much larger premises further up the Walk. Girls like Amanda Knott (from my dancer past) would breeze in, and her friend Caroline Coon. Donald Gardner would turn up, wild-eyed and wild-haired, and while I distanced myself from the Beats – being New York School-orientated back then – I always admired Donald's unwillingness to conform, his intensity. Meanwhile Bernard looked after us all. He sold poets' manuscripts to the University of Texas for significant money. Certain poets created manuscripts after having written the poem in order to take advantage of this lucrative market. Edward Lucie-Smith was editing the Turret pamphlet series for Bernard. Red wine flowed on Saturday afternoons. Peter Porter would hold forth there and Martin Bax would come along and Brian Patten – Bernard was supportive of us all.

I would go and visit Marianne Faithfull (she and I had starred in a school opera back in my schooldays in Reading and we had remained good friends). Mason Hoffenberg would be staying with her, who had co-authored *Candy* with Terry Southern. He said he had written all the dirty bits for Terry. Marianne had read for me at the *Oz* benefit which I organised at the ICA. She gave us a marvellous rendition of 'The Tiger' by Laura Riding. She was a friend of all the beats – Ferlinghetti, Corso, Ginsberg – and always encouraged my poetry.

I edited a small anthology of *Erotic Lyrics* for Studio Vista, and kept wanting to buck the trend towards conformity that I sensed in the poetry world. I was becoming more and more immersed in abstraction. Peter Logan had created a marvellous kinetic sculpture that raised or lowered its arms, which were twelve blue poles. I created *Latissimus Blue*, a choric piece for this that was read in conjunction with the sculpture in Derek Jarman's studio in Bankside, looking out on Tower Bridge. Readers raised or lowered their voices in accordance with the movements of the arms. Peter's brother Andrew was creating wonderfully camp events, one of which involved a half male/half female costume. In winter, the loft was so cold that Derek slept in a greenhouse he had erected in the middle of it. One floor below, Stephen Cripps was pioneering his art in the medium of explosives. The fire brigade were avid followers of his performances. It's a wonder Bankside didn't go up in smoke.

There were lots and lots of parties, and there was always this difference between designer parties and art parties. The designers wore gear that matched that of their partners, so they sort of came in duplicate. The artists were uniformly individuals. I used to favour crocodile platforms, orange dungarees with tin gold stars down their sides and a wide-collared yellow shirt. I did a creative writing workshop for Paul Buck in Wormwood Scrubs and was impressed by one of the Great Train robbers, who read out a ballad inspired by the exploit. Otherwise there were more readings in galleries, notably another choric text (*Solid as Solid*) devised for Ed Meneely's sculptural abstract paintings that took place at the Whitechapel, and a reading with my wife Signe of an erotic text (*Oslo* – later published by Calder and Boyars) to accompany kinetic panes created by Robert Janz in his studio in the old dairy in Prince of Wales Crescent, between Kentish Town and Chalk Farm.

The Dairy was a magical place. Upstairs the London Film Co-op showed the best of material film – David Larcher, Peter Gidal,

Michael Snow and Malcolm LeGrice – the events well organised by Annabel Nicholson who was creating her own expanded cinema and performances. I loved her piece in which she threaded film through a sewing machine and then through a projector, so that the image (of her working at a sewing machine) became progressively punctured. Downstairs, in Janz's studio, when my wife was pregnant with our daughter Storm, I created *Birth Ballet Choral* – a text for pregnant ladies (the text is called *'Scape*), and a large number of pregnant women turned up to participate while Heathcote Williams writhed on the floor attached by the feet to the wife of John Sharkey – this was their version of an oracular snake, I guess, with two heads, and these became progressively bitchier towards each other as the event progressed. Meanwhile pregnant ladies were spinning slowly and serenely with red umbrellas in the next room, and were every so often enclosed in vertical sheets on poles: sheets with red and blue stripes which I had brought back from Iowa.

It was at this time that I founded *Wallpaper* magazine with 11 other editors. Half the editors appeared in an issue, while the other half busied themselves in the production of that issue. Each had a slot, in which you could put your art, music or poetry. The magazine consisted of creative work. There were no essays or reviews. You could get someone else into the magazine if you gave up your own slot. It ran for about six issues. It had wallpaper covers, from end-of-stock rolls.

Then in 1974, I founded The Ting: Theatre of Mistakes, with a first performance at The Artists Meeting Place – run by John Sharkey – in Covent Garden. But that adds another chapter to the story.

Hackney Stopover: Rage in the Eastern Heaven

Iain Sinclair

Albion Village Press was a mistake, I felt. At the time, 1970. And now, worse. The episode is fixed, anthologised, nibbled at by the outreaches of academia; catalogued and assigned a market value. The mistake was the name, the brand. I was never comfortable with it. Two elements of the three grated. The Blakean aspect of "Albion", as aboriginal giant, emanation of place, was contaminated by BNP cells operating behind dubious bookshops with that nameplate. And the "Village" thing was almost as bad, the notion that some accidental Georgian survivor-square is set apart from the sprawl, protected from a threatening otherness. A clod of Deep England, grounded in a city of difference, sustaining property values, restoring original features, and doing a bit of volunteer weeding in the communal garden. In the next decade, when besuited greed, self-interest and paranoia, swaggered from the cave, Village became a catch-all term applied to any secure development within a mile of a public park or no-longer-working canal. The "Press" bit I was happy with: a proper artisanal backstory, with a hint of grape-squeezing, getting the juice from bitter olives.

When I came back to under-the-radar publishing in the Eighties, notebook recoveries in give-away editions of fewer than twenty copies, I traded under some variant of Hoarse Commerce as my flag of convenience. Which felt much better. I instant-printed booklets in as many copies as there were potential readers. For the last one in the series, *Autistic Poses* (1985), I produced ten copies – which was probably an optimistic estimate. But that was fine, I was happy with the name of the press. "Albion's Circumference was Clos'd." One Hoarse Commerce item, Douglas Oliver's *Penniless Politics* (1991), on the back of an extravagant *Guardian* enthusiasm by Howard Brenton, required a second visit to the print shop to supply demand. This was never the intention. The idea was to get the stuff out, fast and clean, and as close to free as possible. Like a letter with live content. It was never part of the plot to become – as it turned out – a staging post towards a visible edition from Bloodaxe. But I was happy for Doug.

Publication in the early Seventies was part of a process of testing a way of living, sharing houses, keeping 8mm diary films, taking on casual jobs in promising locations, and grappling very slowly and laboriously with place, a specific locality. Albion Village Press was, at the start, a group venture: hence the name. Two collaborators from earlier Dublin projects – films, magazines, happenings – were significant players in the launch. Renchi Bicknell, who was coming back to painting, a flurry of intense and self-questioning activity in the wake of acquiring new space, provided images, ideas, arguments. Tony Lowes, who passed through, stepping aside from his worldwide travels in a flurry of phone-calls and herbal smoke clouds, brought anecdotes of the New York scene of the early Sixties, along with transatlantic can-do energy – and funds.

Living in Dublin for four years kept us at a certain distance from what can now be seen as the beginnings of "The British Poetry Revival" (Eric Mottram) or *The Children of Albion* (Michael Horovitz). Neither were we part of that useful adventure in correspondence, the circulation of *The English Intelligencer.* Or the fraught weekend gatherings of warring tribes in Northumberland cottages: Cambridge formalism, Newcastle wildboy. Renchi knew Horovitz and was a friend and travelling companion of Pete Brown. He met Ginsberg in Liverpool. In 1967, I spent a few weeks making a documentary film about Ginsberg, at the time of *The Dialectics of Liberation* circus at the Roundhouse in Camden Town. From Ireland, I made occasional contact with publications like the *Transatlantic Review*, where Burroughs appeared from time to time. I exchanged postcards with the poetry editor, B.S. Johnson. Geographically, being a step closer to the USA, our gaze wandered to the western horizon. Independently of the treaties being tested from Bristol, Cambridge, London, Newcastle, we discovered Black Mountain College, and chased down fugitive publications by Charles Olson, Robert Duncan, Edward Dorn and the rest. Publishing Burroughs gave me the material to effect an introduction to Barry Miles at the Indica Gallery and, later, the Southampton Row bookshop; as well as Better Books in Charing Cross Road and Bernard Stone's poetry-heaped hutch, off Kensington Church Street. *Second Aeon*, edited by Peter Finch, out of my natal city Cardiff, was a good notice-board on which to discover what was going on, and to make contacts. It was inspirational to have the example of Fulcrum, Goliard, Trigram.

Beautifully crafted books by Tom Raworth, Lee Harwood, Roy Fisher, David Jones, Basil Bunting and many of the best Americans. Along the way, I met some of the publishers, independents like Stuart Montgomery and Asa Benveniste. And I became aware of the fertile, multidisciplinary piracies of Jeff Nuttall and Bob Cobbing.

The starting of a small press had a direct relationship with moving to a particular area of London, getting to know printers who were setting up a business in a narrow house close to Balls Pond Road and tucked beside a Jewish burial ground. I had twelve ring-bound folders of material accumulated in the Sixties, but very little of it seemed to fit the new project. I wanted to call this first gathering, *Kitchen Poems*, in honour of the place where we did most of our talking, door open, iron stairs descending into wilderness garden: but that title was taken. As I discovered when I began to explore the poetry shelves of a great new resource, Compendium Books, just up the road from Camden Market. A pleasant hop on the Northern Line.

I met Brian Catling at the North-East London Technical College and School of Art in Walthamstow, where I was teaching a part-time film course to a wildly disparate collection of academic dropouts, crushed-velvet chancers, and unsponsored visionaries. Even as a student, Catling appeared fully formed. Films had been made on his own terms: static camera, projectile vomiting, flying helmets, pyjamas. And now he decided that he would produce a book of poems. I didn't have much choice in the matter: I recognised a notable independence of mind, his own twist on the world. That first book, *Necropathia* (1971), with its green paper and smudgy images of Camberwell bondage, became part of a murder trial in Leeds; but that's another story.

Catling was generous enough to sleep on our floor every Friday night, after pub, and meal, and crash-out Euro-art TV film. He would progress through the Kingsland Waste Market on Saturday morning, scouting for bits of old iron, scrap that might be useful for installations or toys or set designs. He knew how he wanted his books to look.

I came across poems by Chris Torrance in many places, but most frequently in *Second Aeon*. I liked what he did: the shapely language, the conversational ease of performance (crafted) – and again, like Catling, that self-sufficiency. The clincher was J.H. Prynne's tribute to *Green Orange Purple Red* in the Autumn 1969 issue of *Grosseteste*

Review. "The singing voice of such persuasive and dilated movement has not for a long time been heard in the land. It is here covert, aware of distance held off by a species of pearly haze, small faces of the actual suddenly but without surprise revealing an intimate curve… The sacred pornography of the hapless face is delivered up in that most delicate oriental drunkenness last found in the notebooks of Coleridge."

I was out of the door, on the road, back home to Wales. I walked over the hills, through decommissioned mines, conifer plantations, midge clouds, sunburn, blisters, rusty streams, bubbling tarmac, to Torrance's Neath Valley farmhouse. It was an excitement to make contact with what was already a very active network, the magazines and contributors with whom Chris had been involved, his transmigrations from Carshalton to Bristol to Wales. Another place-inspired sequence, *The Magic Door*, would balance the metropolitan excavations I was picking at, and the darker alchemy of Catling. I'm always happy with triptychs, the three-card trick: now we had it. The Press had a purpose, for a few years, helping to put out whatever Catling and Torrance wanted to do. And beyond this, I was delighted to be able to publish Prynne's *A Night Square* – as part of a diurnal sequence; with other elements already taken on through independent presses run by poets, John James and Barry MacSweeney.

Even the limited distribution of Albion Village Press titles, through postal contacts and Compendium, led to meetings with other poets and invitations from Eric Mottram to read at King's College or one of his poetry conferences. There was something of the flavour of the years after the English Civil War, with ranters and levellers, schisms and splits, and Earl's Court poetry wars. I met and read with a number of London-based poets: Allen Fisher, Bill Griffiths, MacSweeney (Londoner by current migration). I also established fruitful exchanges and correspondence with the other active nexus, Cambridge: Prynne, Andrew Crozier, Peter Riley, Doug Oliver. Visits. House swaps. And many letters. MacSweeney met Torrance for the first time in Albion Drive. They forged an immediate alliance.

The civic exhaustion, disenfranchisement, petty council corruption, strikes of that dim era: they helped to form a microclimate in which guerrilla publishing thrived. Operators from the Sixties attempted new engagements with poets who wanted to get things moving, *now*, in the spirit of postal art and Arts Lab spontaneous performance. There was confusion, mess, vanity, incompetence, and much else; along with risk, excitement, fair exchange. And some genius. Some brilliance. For me, this was the time when it happened.

Brixton, Wivenhoe, Gonville & Caius

TONY LOPEZ

My way into contemporary poetry was quite haphazard I think –
mainly because I didn't go to university at the usual age, in fact I didn't
expect to go at all, but went into another kind of scene completely.
It was a very colourful time and a big social experiment. I remember
one day at a friend's house in Bath I was shown a circular visual poem
like a mandala of the word "swallow" that she had made in a poetry/
art workshop. We were fans of the Incredible String Band, so I was
interested when I heard that Thomas A. Clark, who had read at this
event, was in the Incredibles' scene. I got his little book *The Secrecy
of the Totally* and the magazine *bo heem e um* both printed by Charles
Verey's South Street Publications.[1] This was in the late sixties, the first
things that I wrote and made public were for festival events dreamed
up by the Bath Arts Workshop and the Natural Theatre Company. I
had left home in a hurry taking almost nothing but after two or three
years when I decided to focus on writing it was obvious to move back
to south London and get on with that.

I lived with Mary French (she was a student at Wimbledon School
of Art and later a professional illustrator) and tried various jobs while I
wrote most of the time and sent things out to magazines and publishers.
We collaborated on book and print projects. I can't remember where I
got hold of the magazine *Second Aeon*, but that was my first source of
wider information and it gave me a sense of what was possible. I was
trying on all fronts really, sending poems and stories to all kinds of
magazines, book manuscripts to publishers, also getting work printed
and selling it door to door. I think the first poetry I had published was in
an anthology called *Next Wave Poets*; I sold stories to the London daily
newspaper the *Evening News*.[2] Paul Brown who lived in Peckham Rye
published a large format visual poem of mine in his Transgravity series.
In 1972 he edited and published the Dada-Surrealist anthology *These
are Also Wings*. I worked at a small factory moulding resin products,
this was a really awful job in conditions that wouldn't be legal now. I
had to bolt the moulds together leaving the top open and then mix two
reacting liquids and bolt the top on quickly before the mix blew out.

You just couldn't get it done on time every time. The fumes were very bad; I had some serious health problems arising from that work.

So I went to Kingston to get printing done and saw a poster for a poetry reading at the Art School, part of the Polytechnic. I met the organiser Ian Robinson and the reader Lee Harwood; both of them became long-term friends. Ian used the printing facilities at Kingston to produce his magazine *Oasis* and Oasis Books.[3] I helped with this publishing venture, editing and learning about the homemade production techniques: laying out body text typeset on an IBM golf ball machine and making headings with Letraset. Ian got me paid work at the Poly making posters for various musical events; Mary designed covers for Oasis Books. My first book was published by Oasis.[4]

It was some time later when we lived in Tooting that I started to go to the Poetry Society in Earls Court Square. There I soon met Bob Cobbing, Asa Benveniste, Eric Mottram, cris cheek, Harry Fainlight, Lawrence Upton, Clive Fencott, Bill Griffiths, Jeff Nuttall, Barry MacSweeney, Elaine Randell, Allen and Elaine Fisher, Kirby Malone, Martin Booth, Anthony Rudolf, Andrew Crozier, Pierre Joris, Paige Mitchell, Robert Vas Dias, Nicki Jackowska, Anthony Barnett, George MacBeth, Peter Philpott and surely others I don't now remember. I saw readings by many poets including Hugh MacDiarmid, F.T. Prince, Carl Rakosi and Basil Bunting. As I remember it, we mostly hung out two doors along the road at the White House Hotel because it had a bar. I came to realise how different groups in poetry despised each other with a sort of rabid fervour; at that time I hadn't heard of a legitimation crisis. On Saturdays I sometimes went to Bernard Stone's bookshop in Kensington Church Walk; there you could drink free wine and talk poetry. He published Turret Books, including Harry Fainlight and Eric Mottram.[5] I also joined in with the pub readings scene in Croydon and at the Crown and Greyhound in Dulwich.

Out of these many meetings and contacts I became good friends with Allen Fisher and with Eric Mottram. Allen lived nearby; he was producing mimeo work and his place was packed with all sorts of artwork, books and music. Eric taught at King's College and he introduced me to poetry by various American poets I hadn't read and to modern music. I had work published in Eric's *Poetry Review* and later in Allen Fisher's book series New London Pride. I learned to print offset litho in the basement of the Poetry Society thanks to Bob Cobbing who used the equipment to print Writers Forum books as well as *Poetry Review*.

It was around this time that I sold my first novel to New English Library (NEL) Ltd.[6] The book was a speculative fiction imagining a world taken over by an invented cult based on aspects of the Moonies and Scientology. When I had just signed with NEL at Barnard's Inn in Holborn I walked into a nearby agent's office and asked for their help. That was when I met Richard Parker of Campbell, Thomson and McLaughlin who was my agent for the next few years. Dot Houghton at NEL asked for fiction on motorcycle gangs, erotica, horror (they wanted ghouls), and when the film *The Sting* was released they wanted gangsters. So I bought some gangster biographies from a second hand bookshop and got on with it: pasting in episodes from non-fiction sources, writing very fast. This time the contract (a four-book deal) went through my agent and I got a reasonable advance, translation rights were also sold to different regions.[7]

When I had just finished these books I became ill with breathing problems and strange restlessness, was unable to sleep because of short-ness of breath, and then quite suddenly a lung collapsed. I was in hospital for a while and came out unstable, suffering from anxiety. I was put onto sickness benefit for depression; my marriage broke up and I found myself begging places to stay. John Stathatos, who translated Greek poetry and also helped editorially with Ian's *Oasis*, put me up for a while. I went to New York and stayed in the USA for a few weeks, travelling also to Boston, Toronto and Montreal. In Manhattan, with an introduction from Lee Harwood, I visited John Ashbery and David Kermani. This was in 1976 the bicentennial year; John had just won all three major US prizes for his book *Self Portrait in a Convex Mirror*. He showed me around in New York including where Frank O'Hara used to live, and introduced me to Kenneth and Janice Koch. John's partner David Kermani was at that stage working on the Ashbery bibliography. It was John who said to me, "Don't they pay you to go to college in England? You should go if you get the chance". He put me in touch with Peter Ackroyd who gave me some reviewing work for the *Spectator*, and I asked Eric Mottram to give me a reference for university applications. I didn't have the proper credentials for most places but at

Essex I was accepted as a mature student based on a writing sample and an interview. I worked as a proof-reader for science-abstracts journals, and then in production at Pan Books.

Paul Brown and I started as Essex undergraduates at the same time. We worked together to put on poetry events and organised a Festival based on our London contacts. We invited readings by David Gascoyne, Iain Sinclair, Harry Guest, Lee Harwood, Allen Fisher, Bill Griffiths, Tom Raworth, Barry MacSweeney and many others. Also involved with writing at Essex at that time were Ian Davidson, Lucy Ellman, Jeremy Reed, Anthony Barnett, Ralph Hawkins, Charles Ingham and David Barry. Michael Hamburger was a visiting professor; Tom Raworth had been on the translation MA and came to stay when he read. I travelled for readings, mostly London and the Southeast but also to the Northeast where Ric Caddel arranged tours including Colpitts and Morden Tower. Later I published a book with Pig Press.[8] I saw Andrew Crozier when he turned up at Essex every so often for examining. Douglas Oliver had just given up his lectureship there to concentrate on fiction. I think it was Peter Ackroyd who gave me a copy of *The Harmless Building*, a favourite book.[9] Once I got a motorbike I could visit Brightlingsea and go sailing in the Colne estuary with Doug. Paul and I shared a house with other students, but from about halfway through the second year he was mostly in Brick Lane London with his partner Maggie. He later worked in a bookshop there. In the summer of 1979 I went on my little motorbike to Stonypath to meet Ian Hamilton Finlay and see his work.

Impressed with what Doug Oliver, Andrew Crozier and Peter Ackroyd had said about Jeremy Prynne and having read *Brass* and *Kitchen Poems,* I went to Cambridge in 1980 to work on modern poetry for a PhD. I had a studentship at Caius. Tom and Val Raworth were living in Ditton Fields, and I soon got to know Peter Riley, Ian Patterson, Nigel Wheale, John James, Denise Riley, Wendy Mulford, and Peter Robinson. I first met Robert Creeley in Jeremy Prynne's rooms. While in Cambridge I made performance art, the first event was at King's College and then others in Liverpool Art School, Edinburgh Fringe, Oval House London, Cockpit Theatre London, and the Melkveg in Amsterdam. In London I got to know Ken Edwards, Frances Presley, Robert Sheppard, Gavin Selerie, David Chaloner, and John Welch around this time, and I was in touch with Eric Mottram, David Miller, Allen Fisher, Pierre Joris, and Iain Sinclair. I think it was at the V & A that I first met Jonathan Williams and Tom Meyer through Eric. The Cambridge Poetry Festival brought in all sorts of people, and the fringe was even more interesting. It was getting married to Sara and having a first child on the way that made me focus on finishing the PhD. We finally moved away in 1986 when I got my first academic job.

NOTES

[1] Thomas A. Clark, *The Secrecy of the Totally* (1969); *bo heem e um*, edited by Thomas A. Clark (1967-68).

[2] Desmond Hertzberg (ed), *Next Wave Poets* (Next Wave Publications, 1969).

[3] *Oasis* ran from 1969 to 1983 and from 1991 to Ian's death in 2004. From 1983 to 1991, it combined with Robert Vas Dias's *Atlantic Review* to form *Ninth Decade*.

[4] Tony Lopez, *Hide & Seek* (Oasis, 1973).

[5] Harry Fainlight, *Sussicran* (Turret Books, 1965); Eric Mottram, *Shelter Island & the remaining world* (Turret Books, 1971).

[6] *The Second Coming* (New English Library, 1975).

[7] These were published as *The Hoods – Executioner* (1975), *Bootlegger* (1975), *Politician* (1976) and *Dealer* (1976) – under the name Vincente Torrio.

[8] Tony Lopez, *A Handbook of British Birds* (Pig Press, 1982).

[9] Doug Oliver, *The Harmless Building* (Ferry Press, 1973).

King's College and the PCL Poetry Conferences

ROBERT HAMPSON

I arrived in London in September 1967 to start an English degree at King's. I already had a fairly detailed knowledge of English poetry from Chaucer and the *Gawaine* poet through to the Victorians and some grounding in Latin poetry (with Virgil and Catullus as particular favourites). My knowledge of contemporary poetry was based on the *Critical Quarterly* (which meant Lowell, Berryman, Plath, Gunn), the Penguin Modern Poets series, Radio 4 (probably still 'The Home Service'), and the Liverpool Poets (Henri, Patten, McGough) – with some awareness of Ginsberg and Ferlinghetti from the presence of City Lights books in Liverpool bookshops. As an undergraduate, I encountered the work of Pound, Eliot, and Olson; I heard Cobbing read at King's – and, again, at an all-night poetry reading at the Round House, Chalk Farm, where Adrian Henri was also on the bill with his band; and I had been introduced to the work of Lee Harwood and Paul Matthews by my friend Lindsay Badenoch.

Some time in 1972, after my return to King's from an MA in Toronto, where (through my Bengali friends Manub and Himani Bannerji) I had been introduced to the poetry of Rilke, Lorca, Rimbaud, Verlaine and Denise Levertov, I got together with two other King's graduates, Peter Barry and Ken Edwards, and arranged to meet regularly to discuss our work.[1] Out of this workshop grew the magazine *Alembic*. Since my return from Canada, I was also involved with a Liverpool-based multi-media group Zoom Cortex as roadie, bouncer, stand-in light-show operator, and (for one verse only) lyric writer.[2] I also had good friends in the London University Drama Society, Nona Sheppard and Robert Snell, through whom Ken, Peter and I put on a couple of readings and a multi-media performance piece, based on Ken's short story 'Jasper Dean's Final Statement', "a sound collage of poetry, rock and increasing entropy", which included simultaneous performance of texts, discontinuous question and response, back-projections, sound effects and music from the guitarist Keith Washington.[3] At Bernard Kelly's invitation, we did a further performance at his reading series at The Enterprise, Chalk Farm.

We attended readings (particularly at the revived Poetry Society), gave readings (at open mic events at the Troubadour and elsewhere), and even co-organised a series, 'Future Events', with Mike Dobbie and Ulli McCarthy at the White Swan, Covent Garden, the venue later to be used by Sub-Voicive.[4] We extended our networks locally through the Poetry Society, the Association of Little Presses, the London Poets Co-op – and had gradually become aware of a wider national and international field of small presses, little magazines, "experimental" poetries. Thus *Alembic* 2 had included work by Mike Dobbie and Ulli McCarthy; *Alembic* 3 had included not just London-based poets like Paul Brown and Allen Fisher, but also work by Lee Harwood and Jeff Nuttall; by *Alembic* 4, we included work by a range of British poets – Allen Fisher, Roy Fisher, Jeremy Hilton, Bernard Kelly, Eric Mottram – but also American poets – Geoffrey Cook, Emanuel Ro and Alan Davies.[5]

An important input into my own poetry education in this period came from three large-scale conferences organised by Eric Mottram in conjunction with Roger Guedalla and Chris Brookeman at the Polytechnic of Central London. The first of these, the Modern British Poetry Conference in October 1974, consolidated my sense of being involved in a significant contemporary movement that had developed out of early-twentieth-century modernism: the mainstream of twentieth-century poetry hadn't simultaneously climaxed and ended with *The Waste Land*, but had continued running "underground" (as far as official British verse culture was concerned) ever since – not only through Pound (who had just recently died), whose work had been kept in public view through Faber, but also through David Jones, Hugh MacDiarmid and Basil Bunting – two of whom read at this first conference. In addition to MacDiarmid and Bunting, the conference included an older generation of poets – Jim Burns, Harry Guest, Mike Shayer and Gael Turnbull, the last of these known to me as the editors of *Migrant* and the publishers of Roy Fisher's *City* – and a number of younger poets: Andrew Crozier, John James and John Hall, whom I thought of as Cambridge poets; Lee Harwood, Bill Griffiths and Paul Brown, whom I thought of as London poets; and Ken Smith and Paul Evans.[6] As well as the age-range, there was a geographical range and a diversity of poetics. What was missing, of course, was any women poets. I attended the three days of readings, but didn't actually speak to any of the poets.

The second conference, in 1975, was called *Poetry of the Americas*, and was organised by Chris Brookeman. Unlike the previous conference, which had consisted entirely of a series of readings, this included lectures, seminar discussions, and interviews as well as readings. It began with three talks on the poetry of the Caribbean, Mexico and Cuba by Edward Brathwaite, Homero Aridjis and Nicolas Guillén respectively (the last by video), followed by Will Rowe in conversation with Rodolfo Hinostroza about the connections between Latin American poetries and English and North American poetries. The second part of the programme included readings by Edward Brathwaite, Martin Carter, Linton Kwesi Johnson, Homero Aridjis, Rodolfo Hinostroza, Michael McClure and Jerome Rothenberg. McClure and Rothenberg were also "in conversation" with Mottram. Again, no women poets were on the programme. In addition to the impact made by the performances by Rothenberg and McClure, one of my clearest memories of this event is Bernard Kelly introducing himself to a somewhat puzzled McClure as his "British publisher" – on the basis of pirating some of his work. The conference booklet consisted of a lengthy essay by Mottram, 'Entrances to the Americas: Poetry, Ecology, Translation', which begins by citing Octavio Paz's "in writing an original poem we are translating the world, transmuting it" before addressing translation as "the means of moving between languages and cultures". The body of the essay is taken up with an account of three exemplary magazines, *El Cornu Emplumado* and *Io* and *Alcheringa*, and their engagement with translation and ecology across a range of cultures.[7] Grossinger's 'Oecology Issue' of *Io* (1970), for example, demonstrated a "whole earth" consciousness and insisted on our responsibility for the ecosystem; while subsequent issues, like *Alcheringa*, involved "the archaic & primitive as models of basic nature-related cultures". Towards the end of the essay there is a celebration of Margaret Randall's life and work as an outstanding exemplification of "how poetry necessarily enters the political". As with other works by Mottram, the essay presents an immense range of material (including a two-page list of "additional works for study") as part of that necessarily political role of poetry, which was the context in which my own work was situated.

The third conference was two years later in June 1977. This "British Poetry Conference" returned to the format of the first: a series of readings by a range of poets – including even one woman, Elaine Feinstein. The conference theme – set out in Mottram's catalogue essay – was 'Inheritance Landscape Location', and the poets were even more geographically diverse than in the first conference. In addition to the London poets (Allen Fisher, Bill Griffiths, Lee Harwood, Iain Sinclair, B. Catling, Chris Torrance and Mottram himself), there were contingents from Wales (J. P. Ward, Peter Finch, John Freeman), Scotland (Edwin Morgan, Tom Leonard), the North-East (Barry MacSweeney, Tom Pickard) and elsewhere (Jim Burns, Roy Fisher, David Tipton, Jeff Nuttall, Ken Smith, and Colin Simms). Interestingly, with the exception of Feinstein, the connection with Cambridge seems to have been dropped. At the time, the conference confirmed my sense of "London poetry" as part of, and open to, a range of poetry practices. (Indeed, in the listing above, some of the geographical designations are somewhat arbitrary, shifting between place of birth and current residence.) In retrospect, the absence of Cambridge poets (with one exception) suggests that this was a period when London and Cambridge poetries were not on speaking terms. The fact that "British Poetry" is represented almost exclusively by white men at both the 1974 and 1977 conferences reflects the dominance of this group in experimental poetry in this period. I have a memory of standing in a Baker Street pub after one of these conferences: Mottram, Cobbing and Nuttall were standing together, men of a similar age and physical stature, and I remember thinking how they each subtended a particular field of contemporary London poetry through King's, through Writers Forum, and simply through dynamic presence.

NOTES

[1] Another King's graduate, Kathie Edwards, was also invited to the first meeting, but she did not attend any further meetings.

[2] For Zoom Cortex, see Adrian Henri, *Total Art Environments and Happenings* (Thames & Hudson, 1974).

---

[3] 'Jasper Dean's Final Statement' was published in *transatlantic review* 53/54 (1976); Keith Washington, another English graduate from King's, played with the band Tintagel.

[4] 'Future Events' ran from November 3 to December 1. The four events featured Allen Fisher and Ulli McCarthy; Peter Barry, Ken Edwards and Robert Hampson; David Miller and Phillip Jenkins; Paul St Vincent (A.E. Markham) and David Ward; Eric Mottram, Paul Gogarty and Mike Dobbie.

[5] For more about *Alembic*'s publishing history, see David Miller and Richard Price, *British Poetry Magazines 1914-2000* (British Library/Oak Knoll Press, 2006), p.127; Wolfgang Görtschacher, *Little Magazine Profiles* (University of Salzburg, 1993) , pp. 163-5; Ken Edwards, 'From *Alembic* to Reality Street Editions' and Robert Hampson, 'Exploring Different Forms and Formats' in Wolfgang Görtschacher, *Contemporary Views on the Little Magazine Scene* (Poetry Salzburg, 2000), 233-64 and 388-424; and Sophie Seita, 'Interview with Ken Edwards and Robert Hampson', *Mimeo Mimeo* 9 (April 2014), 45-65.

[6] The conference ran from 18 to 20 October 1974.

[7] *El Cornu Emplumado*, edited by Sergio Mondragón, Margaret Randall and Harvey Wolin from Mexico City, 1962-1969; *Io*, first issue edited by Richard Grossinger, Lindy Houghy *et al* from Amherst, 1965; *Alcheringa*, first issue edited by Jerome Rothenberg and Dennis Tedlock, 1970.

A Good Decade for Getting Lost:
London in the 1970s

DAVID MILLER

In June 1972 I left my native Australia and sailed to Singapore, and
after a few days there I caught a plane to England, with London as my
final destination. I was intending to stay for six months or so, meet
some of the poets and artists whose work interested me, and then travel
to Japan (where I was hoping to further my involvement with Shin
Buddhism), and return to Australia. I never even made it to Japan.
Instead, London has been my home for the past 42 years.

Amongst the books I'd been reading in Australia were the Fulcrum
Press volumes by Basil Bunting, Lee Harwood, Tom Raworth and Roy
Fisher, and Edward Lucie-Smith's *British Poetry Since 1945* (the 1970
edition). I'd also been reading the Concrete Poetry anthologies by
Stephen Bann, Emmett Williams and Mary Ellen Solt, which included
British concrete poets (and very importantly for me, the American poet
Robert Lax, in the Bann and Solt books – but more on this later). W.
S. Graham, David Gascoyne and David Jones were other poets I was
immersing myself in – I can remember reading Graham on the ship from
Fremantle to Singapore. My reading of contemporary British poetry
ran in parallel with my reading of US and European poetry, and was
fairly diverse, but it already favoured what I tend to call "exploratory"
poetry (in preference to the terms "experimental" or "avant-garde").[1]

One of the first poets I visited was Sydney Carter. Sydney was better
known as a songwriter, but he also published poems (and sometimes his
song lyrics and poems were indistinguishable from one another). I'd
briefly met him in Melbourne when I snuck into a reading he gave at
Melbourne University (which was the sort of thing I did fairly often)
and talked a little with him afterwards. I phoned him shortly after I
arrived in London, and we quickly became friends. Sydney's down-
to-earth approach to spirituality and his emphasis on the absence of
certainty as something that might actually be productive and positive,
were things I could relate to.[2]

I went to see David Jones a couple of times; I not only admired
Jones's poetry and painting, but also his essays and his lettering art. I

talked with him for several hours on both occasions, and found him a gentle and unassuming person. It was a great honour to visit with him. I also got to know Michael Hamburger, whose translations of German poetry I'd been reading. The visual and sound poet Bob Cobbing, very different from either Hamburger or Jones, was someone else I visited in those first few months. Yet having said this, I noticed that Cobbing had a copy of Paul Celan's poems in Hamburger's translation at his home, and the crossover between the textual and the visual in his work was an example of "text and image", just as Jones's lettering art was another form of it. The most important thing about my meeting with Cobbing was that he put me in touch with a friend of Robert Lax's who lived in London, David Kilburn, and Kilburn in turn put me in touch with Lax. (When Cobbing learned how interested I was in Lax, and that my copy of Mary Ellen Solt's *Concrete Poetry: A World View* was back in Australia, he fetched an old copy of the book and ripped the Lax pages out and presented them to me!) Carlyle Reedy was another poet (and artist) I met early on, and we've remained friends to this day. Someone had told me there was a poet who was also a Buddhist, living not that far from me. He was talking about Carlyle, who lived in a squat in an area known as the World's End, between Battersea and Chelsea, while I resided in a decaying Buddhist community in Clapham, the Amitabha Community. I remember Carlyle introducing me to Lee Harwood as her "secretary" at a reading at The Poetry Society shortly after I'd become friends with her – I think I was helping to sort through her poems!

How did I find out about UK poetry and UK (or UK-based) poets at this time? There were other reading series later on, but at that point The Poetry Society, situated in Earls Court, was the main venue. I saw David Gascoyne there, at what must have been his first public reading in many years. (I believe Lee Harwood introduced him.) I also saw Hugh MacDiarmid, who lectured the audience about how supposedly there'd been no great *English* poets in the 20th century, and I was also at a reading by W. S. Graham, who tried to have a bizarre conversation with me about my gloves! (He was very drunk, needless to say.) There were also occasional events at the ICA (I saw Bunting and Denis Goacher there, reading from Pound's *Cantos* in tandem), and Bernard Stone's Turret Bookshop hosted a regular reading series, though I rarely went.

The other places where you could find out about what was happening in poetry were the bookshops – Turret, Compendium (where Nick Kimberley ran an excellent poetry section), and, for a brief time after my arrival, Better Books. Compendium was where I ran into the poet Kris Hemensley for the first time, though this was slightly later on, probably in 1973. While browsing the poetry shelves, I became aware of two men entering this same section, which was by itself in an upstairs room, and then a man and a woman also entering the room. One of the two men said to the other one, "I wonder if there's anything by David Miller here?" Of course I pricked up my ears. Then the man who was with the woman piped up, "Do you know David Miller?" To which came the reply: "I've never met him, but we've corresponded." At this point I introduced myself. The people in question were Kris (who had indeed corresponded with me) and his younger brother Bernard, and Nick Toczek, who had published me in his magazine *The Little Word Machine*, and Nick's girlfriend. Bernard Hemensley later published a booklet of mine, *In the Midst*.

Another place for finding out about poetry and poets was the Arts Council Poetry Library, on Piccadilly. (Years later it migrated to the Royal Festival Hall in the Southbank Centre, and became known as the Saison Poetry Library.) I found out about presses and magazines through the Poetry Library, also. I'd already become accustomed to sending my work to magazines while I was in Australia, and now I began sending to both magazines and presses in the UK.

Alan Clodd of Enitharmon Press became the publisher of two of my first books, *The Caryatids*, a selection of poems, and an essay, *Malcolm Lowry and the Voyage that Never Ends*. I approached Alan quite early on, I would think in 1973, though it took him a while to bring the books out. He'd published Gascoyne, so at the time at least it seemed reasonable to be included in his series, though I think I stuck out like a proverbial sore thumb. I remain grateful that he encouraged me, however. I approached another publisher, Gaberbocchus Press, around the same time about a book I'd written, mostly in prose, called *South London Mix*. After searching around the shelves in Compendium and the Poetry Library for publishers of exploratory prose, I came across some books by someone named Stefan Themerson, published by a press I'd never heard of before – Gaberbocchus. I sent my manuscript to the Gaberbocchus address, and a few weeks later I received a call from Stefan (who ran the press with his artist wife Franciszka). He said they'd read my manuscript and would like to meet me for dinner. So I went over to their place and had dinner with them. At the end of the evening, Stefan said: "We would like to publish your book". I'm still extremely happy that they did.

A notable contact from those days was John Robinson, who ran Joe di Maggio's Press and published the magazine *Joe di Maggio*. I suspect I simply sent some poems to John, and we ended up meeting. John told me there was a poet named Allen Fisher living not too far from me, and suggested I contact him. When I first went to see him, sometime in 1974, Allen was printing out the pages of the first book instalment of *PLACE* – I picked up the pages and read them as they came off the mimeo machine. Allen was living in Balham at that point, and I was still in Clapham. I met Pierre Joris through Allen, when Pierre was living in Tooting, not at all far away, and the design theorist John Chris Jones (though that would have been a couple of years later). John Robinson also suggested I look up Asa Benveniste, whose excellent Trigram Press I already knew about by then. (Asa eventually fell out with me; he was not the easiest person, but then I don't suppose I am, either.) And when Brian Marley came down from Newcastle, I met him at John's. One meeting led to another meeting, one friendship led to another friendship.

It's impossible to write about these years without including some further mention of Robert Lax, even though I didn't meet him in London. I started corresponding with Bob in 1973, and went to visit him in Greece for the first time in the same year. No one else has been as important to me in my writing, and also in my sense of how to live your life if you're a writer, as Bob Lax.[3] The first of several pieces I published in *Poetry Information* was an essay on Bob's poetry, in 1974. As this is an account of people and things in London, I will only briefly mention two other non-London people who were important to me in those days: the Concrete poet, visual artist and maverick architect Mathias Goeritz, who was a great encouragement to me, and the poet and translator John Riley, who I thought was most probably the finest UK poet of his generation. Both Mathias and John became friends of mine.

I also met a number of visiting Australians at this same time – the poet Kerry Leves and the artist Denis Mizzi, most notably. I lost track of Kerry after a short while, but I've remained friends with Denis until the present time, and we've worked together on various publications. It's perhaps worth mentioning that a friend of Kerry's took me to see the poet and novelist Rosemary Tonks. I had a copy of Peter Whigham's translations of Catullus with me. She asked me if they were any good. I said, "Well, William Carlos Williams thought so." "That doesn't count for much," she responded. Not an especially felicitous meeting.

By 1976 I'd been living in Notting Hill for a year or so, when I sent some work to a magazine called *Alembic,* edited by Ken Edwards, Robert Hampson and Peter Barry, for their fifth issue. I noticed that Ken also lived in Notting Hill, at no distance at all from me, and suggested we meet – or he might have suggested it. The sixth issue of *Alembic*, in Summer 1977, carried a small feature on my work, interwoven with the other contributions. Robert Hampson, whom I saw on a very regular basis by this time, edited the issue.

For a while, Ken, Robert and Peter conducted a reading series in central London, in which I took part. At either this series, or another series that the poet Paul Brown was involved with, at the Enterprise pub in Chalk Farm, I first came to know Philip Jenkins. Philip has a very considerable literary gift – his long poem, *Cairo,* and his book of short fiction, *Travels with Kandy,* are superb and highly singular – and also a great sense of humour. (I remember early on in our friendship he suddenly said to me, "The Apollonian Jenkins is at war with the Dionysian Jenkins", and so they probably were.)

In 1977 Allen Fisher and I collaborated on a book, *The Preparation.* This was probably the height of my friendship with Allen – we were regularly visiting each other in this period and sharing enthusiasms. Allen urged me to send some work to Eric Mottram, whose editorship of *Poetry Review* was about to end. I did, but Mottram didn't really take to it. Although he did invite me to participate in a reading series he organised at King's College London a few years later, I always felt that Eric didn't feel I fitted in with his scheme of how UK poetry should be developing. When Eric told me on one occasion that he didn't think Robert Lax was really a poet, *I knew* I didn't fit in with Eric's scheme of things. I also felt, rightly or wrongly, that he wanted disciples – and as much as I respected him as a scholar, I wasn't disciple material – never have been, never will be. Of course Eric was at the centre of the "Poetry Wars" at the Poetry Society, as was Allen Fisher. Although I read there when Allen invited me and turned down a reading after Allen resigned from the Society, I really had little to do with any of the "warfare" in any direct way.[4]

1977 was also the year in which I began corresponding with Cid Corman – someone else Mottram had little or no time for, except as the editor of the magazine *Origin*. I had made contact with Frank Samperi, after seeing a ludicrously condescending review of his work in *Poetry Information* and, intrigued by the lines of his that were quoted, buying a book of his, *Lumen Gloriae*, and being most impressed. Frank told me that Cid Corman was starting up a new series of *Origin*, and advised me to send Cid some work. This led to my being featured in *Origin* as well as eventually becoming part of Cid's editorial team. It also led to a long friendship, ending only with Cid's death many years later, and it led to friendships with a number of other poets/writers – John Levy, Clive Faust, Will Petersen, John Phillips, Gil Ott, George Evans and, through George Evans, Guy Birchard.

At the end of the 1970s I entered Middlesex Polytechnic, where I studied with the philosopher Doreen Maitre, amongst others, and became friends with fellow student and writer David Menzies.[5] (I'd dropped out of school when I was sixteen, and by 1978 my work record was a joke. For this reason alone I decided I needed to study for a degree.) The next most significant thing from that time was that I made an initial contact with Keith and Rosmarie Waldrop; I sent them a poem sequence called *Primavera* and they published it with their Burning Deck Press. (I later became friends with them when they were living in London for a while, and they were to publish one of my best books, *Stromata*.) Thus we reach the end of my account of the 1970s in London.[6]

Why a good decade in which to get *lost?* I was too involved with writing – and playing music and painting – to ever become interested in a career, and the die was cast in those years. And the idea of poetry as a *career* is just a bad joke, in more ways than one, although I have come across a number of poets I would regard as "careerists". So I was lost to any sort of career. I've never been interested in being anyone's disciple, or belonging to any group, school or movement. Cid Corman's idea of a community of poets, where the connections are to do with deep affinities and very often with friendship, appeals to me – but Cid never meant this with regard to "isms" and certainly not to anything narrow, dogmatic and exclusive, and neither do I. So I was lost to any possibility of belonging to a school or movement. Also, I've never felt the need to write what anyone else thinks I should be writing. So if my writing has not been embraced by more mainstream audiences and critics – and I wouldn't expect it to – then that scarcely makes me want to write differently. But if it's also been ignored by many experimental writers and critics, that doesn't make me want to change what I'm doing, either. There are other possibilities to either the mainstream or the work of the dogmatic experimentalists, and I'm one of the writers exploring some of those possibilities. And of course this means I'm lost.[7]

NOTES

[1] See for example my Introduction to *The Alchemist's Mind: a book of narrative prose by poets*, Reality Street, 2012, pp 34-36.

[2] These tendencies in Sydney's work are exemplified in his books *Nothing Fixed or Final* and *The Rock of Doubt*.

[3] See my essays on Lax in the book *The ABCs of Robert Lax*, ed. David Miller and Nicholas Zurbrugg, Stride, 1999.

[4] For more information on this subject, see Peter Barry, *Poetry Wars: British Poetry of the 1970s and the Battle of Earls Court*, Salt Publishing, 2006.

[5] I've recently published two pamphlets of David's poetry from Kater Murr's Press – *Two Poems* and *From: The Narcosis of Water*. Doreen is the author of *Literature and Possible Worlds*.

[6] For another account of these as well as previous and subsequent years, see my *Autobiographical Essay* in *Contemporary Authors Autobiography Series*, ed Joyce Nakamura, vol 30, Gale Research, 1999, pp 141-160.

[7] Of course the whole mainstream/avant-garde schema can be debated – and I've discussed aspects of it critically myself, while still holding to certain basic distinctions between what might be regarded as mainstream and what might not. See my Introduction to *The Alchemist's Mind*, pp 23-25, 34-36.

My Baptism by Fire

Robert Vas Dias

In the early summer of 1974 my first wife, son, and I booked passage to London on the Soviet ship *MS Mikhail Lermontov* in New York; I'd been born in London but had gone to the States in 1940 and had only been back to England in 1973 to do a series of readings. I was on a one-year poetry grant from the New York State Council on the Arts, while my wife found a place to study at what became the Anna Freud Clinic.

Soon after my arrival in London I'd got to know David Chaloner; he and I admired several of the New York School poets, and we formed a firm friendship. I became dimly aware – though not to the extent of the baptism-by-fire of a few months later – of the cliques and divisions of the British poetry scene, but David was not in the least dogmatic and tended to downplay the schisms and hostility between the factions. He was, however, at pains to explain that, although he was sometimes lumped together with the poets of the Cambridge School, he hadn't attended Cambridge and was only associated with them on the basis of sympathies in the work, friendships, and publications. I knew exactly what he meant, because the milieu in which I functioned in New York was analogous to that which David described: various groupings of "The New American Poetry" – Black Mountain, San Francisco and West Coast, New York School, Beats, Deep Image – were connected by friendships, readings, magazines, correspondence, and similar sympathies, and were united in their distaste of the prevailing orthodoxies of the academic and quasi-academic poets of the establishment. David, who was a professional designer and graphic artist, did the cover of my first book in Britain, *Making Faces*, published in 1975 by John Robinson's Joe DiMaggio Press.

As in New York, where Eli and Ted Wilentz's Eighth Street Bookshop and Frances Steloff's Gotham Book Mart stocked the latest poetry and served as meeting places for local and visiting poets, London's Compendium and, before my arrival, Better Books and Indica, were likewise places where poets congregated and found the poetry, and the ambience, they were looking for. Shortly after I arrived, Pierre Joris, himself a recent emigré from Luxembourg, introduced me to Compendium, where I found the marvellous volumes published by Stuart Montgomery's Fulcrum Press and Nathaniel Tarn's Cape Editions. When I re-started Permanent Press in Britain in 1975 with a pamphlet by Jackson Mac Low, I found a ready outlet for my publications at Compendium.[1]

By the time I came to London the counterculture was definitely a constituent of the living culture, the "British Poetry Revival" (Eric Mottram's term) had arrived, the underground had emerged above-ground, and Michael Horovitz's *Children of Albion* were becoming more widely published (some, like Roy Fisher, Lee Harwood and Tom Pickard, were even elected to the General Council of The Poetry Society). I'd already known about Michael's work – I'd invited him to give a reading in Michigan – and I wanted to familiarise myself with the London poetic *zeitgeist* by going to readings not only at The Poetry Society but also at the various London venues where performance poets like the reggae poet Linton Kwesi Johnson, Benjamin Zephaniah, and John Cooper Clarke filled the halls.

Before my grant ran out, I saw an ad in, I think, *The New Statesman* for the post of General Secretary of The Poetry Society and applied for the position. References were of course needed but, since I'd never worked in Britain, I asked some American poets and the dean of the university in Michigan where I'd been poet-in-residence for three years and where I'd founded and directed two National Poetry Festivals. I was shortlisted and called in for an interview before a committee of the General Council, one of whose members was Roy Fisher, and was notified a few days later that I'd got the job. Among the referees was Allen Ginsberg, who'd sent me a copy of his complimentary letter to the committee; that, and I think the behind-the-scenes advocacy of Eric Mottram, did the trick.

I was let down gently at first into The Poetry Society cauldron, guided by the wisdom, tact and humour of Laurence Cotterell, the chairman. As in the States, there was little or no sustained contact between what could be called the innovative, radical poets of the "left" and conservative poets of the "right wing"; but in fact, I was shocked by the vitriolic hostility of some on the left for those on the right in the General Council, which culminated in a mass resignation some two-and-a-half years later of the radicals, as everyone knows from Peter

Barry's *Poetry Wars*.[2] (Strangely enough, I was never consulted, nor even contacted, by Barry about my role in the *fracas*, which admittedly was mainly to try and hold things together so the Society could continue to function.) I thought that the radicals had shot themselves in the foot by walking out – they no longer had a power-base from which to publish and organise readings and propagate their views, but my sympathies were obviously with them, and I followed the walkout a few weeks later.

I won't go into the often petty and vindictive behaviour of some, a painful experience at the time, particularly falling out with Mottram and Cobbing – with both of whom, incidentally, I fell in with again after a time. The whole experience was made more bearable by the supportive friendship and pragmatism of the late Ian Robinson, editor-publisher of Oasis Books and *Oasis* magazine, who was vice-chairman of the Society.

I must say that both Bob and Eric, for all their prickly natures and sometimes dogmatic pronouncements, were, in their editing lives, generous and encouraging to some poets who "crossed the lines" in their work, Bob in his Writers Forum series and Eric in his editing of *Poetry Review*. Given his strident and intransigent views on the "opposition" represented on the Council, Eric was, I thought, quite eclectic in his editing and did not deserve the disapprobation of his critics, particularly those on the Arts Council, and chiefly Charles Osborne, the Literature Director.

Cobbing, who had an international reputation as a concrete and sound poet, was in my opinion shockingly underrated in his own country.[3] Writers Forum eventually published over 1,000 pieces – OK, some were little more than ephemera, but others were large books, particularly, for example, *Concerning Concrete Poetry*, edited by Cobbing and Peter Mayer.[4] Bob was very much a hands-on poet-artist, often to be found in the Poetry Society's basement print shop running off sheets of design poems, some of which he rescued from amongst piles of waste and rejects on the floor, reworked and absorbed as pages of stapled A4 offset litho books. "Mistakes can be found chance procedures," he said, which I completely understood from having talked and worked with Jackson Mac Low in New York. He encouraged and was frequently assisted by young poets, including Clive Fencott, cris cheek, and Tony Lopez, who originated and ran off their own publications on the Roneo and Gestetner machines. The other task, a herculean one, that Cobbing, Lawrence Upton, Bill Griffiths and others performed, was to design the covers, print, collate, and bind 2,000 copies of the 60-page in-house A4 *Poetry Review*, after the Arts Council reduced its grant to the Society in an effort to force out Mottram and the radicals. This effort lasted for several issues before the mass resignations.

A curious aspect of the London poetry scene at least, was the comparative social isolation of some poets, which was brought home to me when I gave a party for Kenneth Koch at my house after his reading at The Poetry Society. Chaloner had always wanted to meet a certain poet, whose name I've forgotten, and who was at the party; it turned out that this poet lived not a mile away from David's house, and yet for years neither one had managed to bring themselves to the point of arranging a meeting. This was really puzzling to me.

It was disappointing to me as a transplanted Anglo-American that The Poetry Society made little or no effort at that time to attract women on to the Council, which was dominated by men – white, generally middle-class males – and likewise there was no representation of ethnic minorities, male or female.

Since I hadn't grown up in, been educated in, or become part of a poetry scene in Britain when I stepped ashore, the mid-1970s were formative for me as a poet and editor. I had a lot of learning to do in a short space of time. Moreover, being in a paid executive position in a poetry organisation in which I was meant to be even-handed and objective in following the wishes of the Council and, more importantly, had to be seen as such, was not necessarily an advantage in endearing me to either faction. In retrospect, I probably shouldn't have taken the job, though it was that or going back to teaching. Nevertheless, despite the frustrations, it was also exhilarating, and in my parallel existence as publisher of Permanent Press I was able to join in and exhibit with the ALP (Association of Little Presses) which Cobbing and Stuart Montgomery had founded in 1966 and continued in The Poetry Society, and which became annual events at other venues.

Permanent Press issued booklets by American and British poets, including Armand Schwerner, Paul Blackburn, Kelvin Corcoran (his first book, *Robin Hood in the Dark Ages*), Elaine Randell, Edward Dorn and Jennifer Dunbar, Jonathan Griffin, Ralph Hawkins, Clarence

Major, Toby Olson, Nathaniel Tarn and Janet Rodney, and a book of drawings by Ian Robinson. I also edited *The Atlantic Review: New Series*, with the British artist Ian Tyson as Art Editor, and later on *Ninth Decade* and *Tenth Decade,* with Tony Frazer and Ian Robinson. My contribution to these magazines was to obtain work mainly from American poets and to commission some critical writing – from Eric Mottram on the work of Paul Blackburn, for example.

One principle which became increasingly clearer to me was that an arts organisation – or a magazine or small press, for that matter – that accepts largesse from a government agency like the Arts Council (unless it is given unconditionally, for instance to work on a project or collection) not only is beholden to that agency in ways that are not immediately obvious, but becomes dependent on the annual renewal of the grant which, in times of retrenchment, may not happen; the recipient is then liable to fold or drastically curtail its operation. That's one reason I never applied for a grant for my press. The Poetry Society had to sell its spacious building in Earls Court Square when it could no longer afford to keep it up, despite my having gone to some lengths to acquire the freehold; its current quarters function in a much reduced manner.

Notes

[1] Jackson Mac Low, *36th Light Poem in memoriam Buster Keaton.* London & New York: Permanent Press, 1975.

[2] Peter Barry, *Poetry Wars: British Poetry of the 1970s and the Battle of Earls Court.* Cambridge: Salt Publishing, 2006.

[3] As of 1974, he had published or exhibited his work in Argentina, Austria, Belgium, Canada, Czechoslovakia, France, Germany, Italy, Japan, The Netherlands, Spain, Switzerland, Yugoslavia, and the United States.

[4] Bob Cobbing and Peter Mayer (eds), *Concerning Concrete Poetry.* London: Writers Forum, 1978.

The Translation Workshop
and *Ecuatorial* magazine

WILL ROWE

I had read the Penguin Modern Poets (the Lee Harwood and Tom Raworth one hadn't come out yet, that was 1971), plus the usual other more-or-less mainstream stuff, Larkin for example, whom I'd heard Donald Davie lecture on enthusiastically – I found him depressing and couldn't see what the fuss was about. But until I got to Peru I hadn't read Neruda or Vallejo. Back in London, end of sixties, two events shook me up: a performance by Bob Cobbing and a series of seminars on American poetry by Eric Mottram at the ICA. So something else was going on in London. I soon began reading Lee Harwood and Tom Raworth and others – and American poets such as Robert Duncan and Ed Dorn. I met Phil Maillard, then living in East Dulwich, and through him Chris Torrance, who had moved from London to Wales. Hugo Gola and I translated poems from Torrance's *Acrospirical Meanderings in a Tongue of the Time*. A longer term result of these engagements is the anthology of British poetry recently published by Mangos de Hacha in Mexico, which includes Mottram, Torrance, MacSweeney, Raworth, Harwood, and Maggie O'Sullivan.

What led to the idea for a translation workshop came from the experience of translating Peruvian poetry in the late sixties and the people I met in the 1970s when I was teaching at King's College. I had come back from a teaching job in Peru with a bundle of political poetry by contemporary Peruvian poets, among them Javier Heraud and Antonio Cisneros. The Cisneros translations became part of *The Spider Hangs Too Far from the Ground*, a selection of his poems done in collaboration with David Tipton and Maureen Ahern. It was published by Cape Goliard in 1970.

King's College brought me into contact with Eric Mottram and through him with Allen Fisher, Pierre Joris, Ken Edwards and a great many other London poets. The translation of Latin American poetry became part of two decades of conversation with Mottram, who published my translations of Pablo Guevara and Juan L Ortiz in

Poetry Review. We shared an admiration for Latin American guerrilla poets, some of whose work was collected in the Ed Dorn and Gordon Brotherston book, *Our Word: Guerrilla Poems from Latin America,* also published by Cape Goliard in 1970. The immediacy and risk of these poets' engagement was something to take very seriously: it gave a new practical meaning to the Sartrean notion of engagement in a situation that was shaped by the political effects of the Cuban Revolution and which meant putting your life on the line. Mottram wrote an important essay for the Polytechnic of Central London Poetry of the Americas conference of 1975, with the title 'Poetry, Ecology, Translation'. It includes an account of Latin American work available in translation.

There was, at the same time, another group of people in London who were directly involved in Latin American and Spanish poetry: the poets were Juan Antonio Masoliver, originally from Barcelona and teaching at the then Polytechnic of Central London; Hugo Gola, in exile from Argentina; Eugenio Montejo, from Venezuela; Thito Valenzuela, in exile from Chile. In addition, Jason Wilson and Nissa Torrents taught Latin American literature at King's and UCL, respectively. The British poet Anthony Edkins had been translating the Spanish poet Luis Cernuda. Ken Edwards had published *Lorca, An Elegaic Fragment* (Alembic Editions, 1978), a fine response to Lorca materials. I also met Stephen Watts who, apart from translating prolifically from Italian and other languages, was engaged in compiling a huge bibliography of work by British translators. I invited Rodolfo Hinostroza and Enrique Verástegui, two of the most interesting younger Peruvian poets, to come to London to read at King's College in the 1970s.

The Translation Workshop, based loosely around King's College, met fortnightly in the late 1970s and early 1980s. Members included Juan Antonio Masoliver; Jason Wilson who lectured at King's and was an expert in Argentinian poetry; the British poet Anthony Edkins, translator of Luis Cernuda and published by Waterloo Poets; Ulrich Toller, student at King's and German-speaker; William Rowe who also lectured at King's and had translated Peruvian poetry. Hugo Gola visited on occasion. At the meetings we worked on collective versions, which were arrived at via intense discussion of variant readings and renderings. The result was a sense of the poem as a field of micro-decisions. Poems traversed through various modes became enriched in the process though sometimes they also unravelled into unfocused multiplicity and at that point had to be abandoned. The main problem with the collective versions was, I think, that they sometimes lacked the consistency that comes when there's one translator whose own poetic practice informs the work. That's where the collective translation project came up against a limit. Out of that there emerged something like an ideal way of working: after collective discussion, one of the members would then produce a final text. This is probably the main reason why the workshop ended: we had to an important extent exhausted the possibilities of collective work and subsequently most of us continued to work individually, but always with the workshop experience in the background.

The main orientation was towards work in Spanish, by Spanish and Latin American writers, though Rilke and Pavese also figured as well as work by American poets, O'Hara and Ashbery for example, translated into Spanish. The main concern was the radical tradition that in Latin America involved poets such as Osvaldo Lamborghini, Francisco Madariaga, Octavio Armand, Alejandra Pizarnik, and Ernesto Cardenal. From Spain, Lorca, Cernuda and Gimferrer were the main poets.

The Workshop led to the publication of a journal, which was called *Ecuatorial*, after the book by Vicente Huidobro, and in recognition of Jerry Rothenberg's extraordinary 'Cokboy' poem, but which also served as a way of citing a geographical orientation towards the south. The cover of No. 3 (Summer 1980), made by the Portuguese print-maker Bartolomeu dos Santos, who taught at the Slade School, featured a facsimile of Lorca's signature in diagonal, crossed horizontally by a line with "crossing the line" printed immediately beneath it. *Ecuatorial* was a bilingual journal in English and Spanish, published c/o the Department of Spanish at King's College, where Wilson and Rowe (and temporarily, Masoliver) taught. Artist Peter Donelly, partner of Nissa Torrents, made the cover of No. 1. Donelly had done the covers of several of Eric Mottram's books, and Mottram himself contributed to No. 3 with a translation of Lorca's 'Ode to Walt Whitman', produced jointly with Will Rowe. Other work featured included, in No 2, Creeley and Spicer translated by Masoliver, the Argentinian poet Enrique Molina by Edkins, Antonio Machado by Ken Edwards, the Catalan poet Pere

Gimferrer by Arthur Terry, Rodolfo Hinostroza by Will Rowe, and an essay, 'Identity and Translation' by Jason Wilson. No 3 included Clayton Eshleman's translations of César Vallejo, Ashbery translated by the Uruguayan poet Roberto Echavarren, Echavarren translated by Wilson, the Peruvian poet Enrique Verástegui in versions by Rowe, Frank O'Hara by Masoliver, the Argentinian poet Edgar Bayley by Edkins, and articles on the Cuban poet Octavio Armand by Naomi Lindstrom, who taught at the University of Texas at Austin, and by Pierre Joris, living in Tooting at the time, on Paul Blackburn's Lorca translations. There were *Ecuatorial* readings at the Whitechapel Gallery and King's College Readings, several readings of Latin American poetry at the Sub-Voicive series, then organized by Gilbert Adair, and a reading at the ICA to mark the anniversary of the Cuban revolution.

Poetry in the 1970s

STEPHEN WATTS

I began the 1970s in Oxford where I stayed a year, before abandoning it.

In summer 1971 I went to live on North Uist (in the Western Isles). My sense of poetry started in those years, which is why I mention these things. At Oxford it was entirely the bookshops that mattered & in them the access to translations of poets such as Trakl or Rilke or Hölderlin & Celan & mostly via Wittgenstein. I wasn't "reading" English there & I didn't start to write until I had left Oxford well behind. And I cannot recall going to any poetry event or gathering at that time in Oxford at all (later, yes).

On North Uist it was the landscape (its age, beauty & harshness) & the people & behind everything the political history of the Clearances & the historic banning of spoken Gaelic. These things mattered most to me in terms of poetry, these & the reading of Dante. The strengths of the Gaelic tradition in contemporary life & the gash of the landscape. From all this early on I felt that what was "experimental" was rooted in fractured otherness.

When I came back to London to live, first for a few months in 1974 and then permanently from summer 1976, I lived in Whitechapel & Cable Street. It was an intense time, but one also of "misses" or absences. Bill Griffiths was living behind the London Hospital not far from where I was in the mid-70s & I knew nothing of him at the time. Lee Harwood had been living in Cable Street & then Stepney in the mid-60s & I didn't get to know his work until well after the '70s were over. I suppose this is understandable: but we were all living intensely in the geographies of those places right through those years.

What engaged me was the landscape and poverties of Tower Hamlets (the dead docks), and, in political terms, racism (I had many Bangladeshi friends). I consciously eschewed what I knew of English poetries & was "blissfully" unaware of the ructions at the Poetry Society. I simply didn't want to drift towards the surface of mainstream English poetry, and I didn't know enough of the "experimental" zones of work within contemporary English poetry.

What did engage was the energy of the recent Worker Writers movement and the sorts of democracy being practiced particularly at the Basement Writers in Cable Street and Centre-prise in Dalston. Both of these became established from the early 1970s in the wake of the sacking of Chris Searle from John Cass School where he had held poetry classes for school-kids & published their poetry (for which latter outrage he was sacked). Those kids came out on strike for him & that story made it to the front pages of papers (*The Sun* supporting a strike by school kids on behalf of their sacked teacher). I want to stress the Worker Writers' movement (which I was very marginal to) because it has been overlooked & disregarded by more experimental poetry movements. I think what it did in the '70s mattered a lot & that the history of its works & struggles is well worth articulating. But the "non-involvement" & ignorance was mutual & most poets associated with the Worker Writers tended to eschew the experimental (this is to over-generalise, hard not to in a short piece such as this is).

But I wasn't much of a "group" guy & didn't get to the Basement as often as its proximity just up Cable Street should have allowed. I was very involved in reading translated poetry and got my energies and alternative sources to what I felt appallingly as the dryness of English poetry from a whole range of translated poetries (not just European) & from the peopled landscapes of London. And what mattered for those sources in the mid & late '70s were:

- Second-hand bookshops in London & elsewhere: Compendium was key here & the absence of such a bookshop now in London is very painful. But also for instance Dillon's second-hand. And also dedicated places: Hungarian Books in the garage of a house in Kilburn, the Polish Library in Hammersmith, Ruposhi Bangla in Tooting (for Bengali books), SOMA Books near the Elephant & Castle for contemporary & radical Indian poets. All these & others were important places for me & urgent to my sense, at least, of the experimental.

- Access to university libraries. This was very important: in the '70s any member of the public could apply to use university libraries for free. I accessed superb poetries & translations at UCL & SSEES & SOAS & it provided me with worldwide alternatives (what Mandelstam had called a "craving for world poetry"). No university library now is so freely open.

- London's Poetry Library which, for all its "establishment" connections, did provide access to poetry from many & international sources. Also special holdings across GLC Libraries (for instance, Tower Hamlets had the London holdings of French, German & Portuguese books & a Specialist Librarian who took his work seriously).

- Contact with a few people: John Welch for instance, both as poet & small publisher (though I may have got to know him in the '80s & via his work teaching in East London), Tony Rudolf & Menard Press similarly, Richard Leigh, Elizabeth Cook, Marius Kociejowski & others. Though always as individuals rather than as anything of a connected group.

- Bengali (Bangladeshi) poetry in the East End I had much contact with & the energies & recent memories of the 1971 War of Independence & the whole "power" of the Language Movement from 1952. Also Tagore & music. All these also as clear cultural alternatives to the English mainstream.

These fed my very deep need for an alternative to the dry rot of mainstream poetry. What amazes me in retrospect is that I didn't at the time look for alternatives in other streams of English poetry. I simply wasn't aware of what Bill Griffiths or Bob Cobbing or Jeff Nuttall and many others were doing or where they were doing it. I wish I had fed in their work to what I was pursuing via the "liberation of translation" at that time. I didn't at that time have much contact either with Will Rowe at King's, more of a tacit respect. Thus I was reading César Vallejo in the late '70s (books from Compendium) but not interacting with all of this.

What engaged me most was a sort of poetry on the hoof. Not a Poetry Café, but the ordinary poetry of people in cafés & those who needed to eat. The music of Bengali baul singers who could be heard (& the deep poetry of their rhythms) across Tower Hamlets. The example of Sorley Maclean and the fantastic rigours & music of some Gaelic poetry. The examples of Gramsci & Pasolini (though I got to value the latter's work later on). Finding Attila József & Tudor Arghezi in Compendium & in SSEES Library, Faiz Ahmed Faiz & Nâzım Hikmet at Compendium & SOAS. Finding Hugh MacDiarmid's poetry in the Poetry Library in 1977 (vivid memory of this).

A recollection: going to a reading of 5 Hungarian poets (very good poets including Ferenc Juhász & Sandor Weöres) at King's College either in the late '70s or early '80s. Will Rowe might have been there. I think Eric Mottram probably introduced the event. I much enjoyed it. But I didn't "recognise" the English poets (such as Mottram) who were there. Not that I didn't want to, rather that it didn't happen. And it wasn't just me; it didn't happen the other way round either. The poets I knew then were such as David Kessel: who still lives in the East End, a deep and very fine poet to my mind in the breakdowns from his doctoring days and the schizophrenic acuities of his daily practice. I mean this, as I most often do, as solid bodily experience rather than as metaphor. All of this (the landscapes & mental & linguistic stress & much else of lives in the East End) seemed to me to be one root and also the heart of the "experimental". There are a number of poets who have lived in East London for many years & remain hardly known who in my opinion should be far better known: David Kessel, David Amery, Howard Mingham. Harking back to Isaac Rosenberg whom I thought a lot about all through the late '70s as having had the potential of a variant & alternative modernism.

RETRO/PER/SPECK/TIFF 2   Clive Fencott

Read English Version

The text as a site for working from, n
ot as a holder for a programmed readin
g, certainly not as a fixed signifying
machine, but as a catalyst for a way o
f working towards a meaning, not an inevitable meaning, prescribed in hop
e by the author; but the text as a starting point for the performance of
a mea ning: either by a reader in their private space and time or perform
er readers in a public space and time of some realisation in improvised v
ocal performance.

Bill Griffiths would oft
en annotate a text in pe
n or pencil blockin out
text for particular voic
es or annotating lines t
achieve an interplay of
voices, he did this very
quickly as if he knew, h
ad it in mind, how an im
promptu, multi-voice per
formance of the text cou
ld sound. I have example
s such annotations for A
Brief History of the Sol
ar System, Quatermass an
d the Pit, and The Twent

The response, interpretation, pef
formance expected to be, as if, u
nrehearsed, the text handed out o
n the spot, in the moment, allowi
ng no time for read or run throug
h, dumb, silent or otherwise, nothing a
pproximating rehearsal: this true
of both verbal texts with or with
out performance annotations; or a
bstract text-soond compositions.
This role of the text was never v
oiced explicitly at the Tuesday n
ight workshops at the National Pe
etry Centre, no one was ever told
that was the way of working, it j
ust was that way and regular work

lightni
glowers
dieser
Sky sien
ja, dumh,
Blitze,
tubby,
überal
derben
Dom
Paderbo

etc.

y Fifth Anniversary: Six Sections
on the Scheduled Visit of the Quee
n to Pa derborn (quoted in this es
say)
Bob's text-s ts, sounding
interpreted isations of,
lack ink mar ite paper, w
rently freer pretation: b
ot the case e as anythin
do for these nces, it was
v to listen ond to the o
formers: the r of that pa
performance of thet text would eme
rge and would be coherent in some
sense. (Bob's text-sound text 'Int
egration Is Not Enough, 1969, quot
ed here)
Texts could be typed, in the pre-w
ord-processing meaning of the word
, or could be hand written or coll

44 Eager ound tex
45 A bro as vocal
46 After often. b
47 Charl ks on wh
48 He sa ere appa
   for us b in inter
49 The h ut was n
50 They as simpl
   have bee g would
51 A fea performa
   the youn necessar
   and resp
   ther per
   charact e
   rticular
   the sun

shop participants would expect a te
xt to be suddenly thrust into their
grasp and to immediately stand up a
nd perform it without any prior kno
wled ge of the text creator's aesth
etic, political or multivoice inten
ions.
Often the reward for the conscript,
the contexted, was to take away. Tha
t copy, often a new publication. Th
at I believe is how I came to have
two copies of The Horseshoe Falls (
Niaga   ra). I think B
ill g   ave me one to
perfo   rm at the work
shop   and Bob gave m
e one   when I went ro
und t   o his house: v
isits   to Bob's house
almos   t always res u
lted   in leaving wit
a num   ber of ne writ
ers P   orum publicati
ons.
The accoustics of the performance s
pacewould also very definitely affe
ct the performance, and people's vo
ices change a lot in relation to th

aged, could be abstract mimeograph
s reproduced by Bob on his Gestetn
er, the funda
al nature of
texts bein an
diacy that co
mputer based
production ha
s eliminated,
hence the pre
sentation of
this document
as an attempt
to capture so
mething of th
text of the I
970s and to p
resent a text
for both solo
reading and m
ulti-voice pe
fformance.
And the abstr
act text-soun
d as catalyst
for the poem as a performa
nce even made it on to nat
ional TV: see YouTube Bob

e ambient environment and its accou
stics and t he interplay of voices
moving with and against the others:
ment   such
dissonance, harmony, the voices as
imme   much if not more than the text, a g
                reater transient w
                hole leaving the t
                ext behind.
52 In his s   On a tour of North
sees Pope L   America in I982 Bo
wounds his   b and I produced a
ers to Rome   new text-book for
53 In the m   each city by pheto
his army as   copying from exist
54 The meas   ing texts, writing
Detailed questioning   on the way, cuttin
55 The filt s of marks, texture e   g up and collag
ing it kill dges dots and lines,   ing found mater
56 A mob at contrasts, directions
tongue and of readings over the
57 But with two dimensional inksc
and his pow ape of the
58 The pope text: mayb
messengers e suggesti
magne   ng, someho
59 Accompan w stimulat
set out.   ing the, o
60 They cro ften emoti
cheer them onal, voca
            l response
            s, shorn of words, so
            unds of voices uncons
            trained by language,

61 Meanwhile   ing material etc. The b
of his troop   ook would be pe
62 The earth   rformed as a tw
their horses   o voice poem wi
echoes to th   th a member of
                    the audience ch
                    arged with stop
                    ing the 'authors'
                    after a prearrange
                    d time, usually 20

and Clive on The 73 Show i
n 1984: a mass-media maste
r class in text-sound peff
ormance.
The performance, private o
r public, was, is a pshch-
physiological response to

loose...g of the new homage of the Queen,
d of ...rmany.
cultu
ral b...d Obermursberg, perfect, in car.
onds:...n the more north side of the
in co
llaboration with the minutes.

The four
Ram and cat
the text and the co-perfor
mer s, poetry as experienc
; meaning embodied with an
d also beyond words.

Gliding in for the encore
Touch down at the arena
other voices and the
ambient environment:
or, often times, the
holistic view jumps m

beasts of the God
mastiff and bear
But in all cases th
text was a starting
point not a realisa
tion of a set of si
gnifiers for a sp
ecifically meanin
gful outcome; poe
try as an experie
nce for both the
performer and the
perceiver.

However it should be clear
that a text could have bot
h its single author voice

y perception, sounding
now whole forms of bla
ack against white movi

It shouldn't be sup
posed that this way
of working, this at

for consumption alongside   ng across and into eac   titude to the text

The ram it is and now heralded by the loyal remnants first
grinds its horns   trigger happy bayonet crooners in the welcome.
It slews and   shadow of shadows   soldiers around
offering the toy tin soldiers spill in a grinning ring right its fat powers
to the windows   down your front.   of the mill.

its various multi-voice r   hother across the whol   , this contexting;
ealisable potentialities: e plane of the text: e   wa s common, was i
the authored text to more   lse, I drift inwards t   n any way a standa
conventionally read thus   hinking, not thinking,   rd for the text in
complicating the spaee of   of the text or anythin   those times, becau
the text's performable re   g else except, accept   se it wasn't. It w
alisations.   the sound of my voice   as a feature of th
jgjgjgjg is an interestin   and how it sounds with   ose associated wit
example. Despite all the   the other sounds; and   Bob Cobbing and th
texts performed there wer   other ways of working   e workshop, the Ca

in his   along   doubled-over beckonning.
He is shabby   along to your own sweet song   with shit
and   under the black bat king beat winging will not wait
with his gift of away in a royal copulation   the whole garrison.

e no publications as such   into voice from the te   adian sound poets,
; jgjgjgjg was never publ   xt, alternates across   The Four Horsemen,
ished, were never authors   the performance: the wh   and later Owen Sou

in this group.
There was a pu
blished casset
te, soon to be
vinyl ed, but
the t exts the
mselves never became obje
cts of dissemination. Thi
s was discussed, Lawrence
reminded me recently, but
was not an issued acted u
pon. The text was for per
formanc
e. "we
being o
f sound
/ sensi
ng the

ile on inside the perf
ormance, the experience
of, the sounding extra
neous to, enveloping,
almost trivialising th
e text, that the, this

nd, were exponents
of this approach t
ough they didn't t
o my knowledge imp
rovise from abstra
ct texts. It was n

Fank alone

page 16: Section Five

Together, improvised, whisper.

possibilities", a jgjgjgj
g information leaflet pro
claims, was most certainl
y not the worm, was seen
at some distance by those
witnessing the performanc
e, but were never able, a
vailable to be read after
/to-later/wards more stud
ious understanding of the

role of the text accom
plished: noising as a
being
somat
ic in
this
place
of vo
ices.
I alm

ot even a common f
eature of the wide
r international se
und-poetry scene.
This way of workin
g was useed in the
contemporary class
ical world: compos
ers such as Stockh
ausen and Corneliu

page 17: Section Six

piece; now separated from
its text.
The text published would
still be t he text for pe
fformance, all texts, poe
ms, nov
els are Section Three
to a gr
eat exten completed by th
e reader, but t he text,
text-sound text, the text
appropriated for multi-
voice performance requi
res considerable reinte
rpretation no t just a
but still mindful readi
ng. Publishing such tex
ts for performance is m
ore akin to music publi
shing, sheet music that
is, than conventional p
oetry publishing.
When I worked with free
improviser Steve Moore, I
would improvise using a r
ange of texts, computer p
rint-outs in the early 19
80s, smudgy silver adn gr

ost always had a sense
of the character of th
e piece in its particu
lar performance and wh
at would be appropriat
e or innapr
opriate to
add to it:

Silent

often the innapropriat
was appropriate and the
appropriate inappropri
ate,
a qu
esti
on o
f mu
t pe
rfor
manc
e int
uith
on f
ar m
ore than rational piec
e-making; though the l
atter strategy was emp
loyed at times. Perfor
mance in this context

s Cardew being exa
mples. In October
1970 I took part i
n the first peffor
mance of the latte
r's The Great Lear
ning paragraph 4,
for chorus (shouti
ng and playing rid
ged instruments or
notched ones; sono
rous substances, r
attles or jingles)
and organ, in St.
Pancras Church, Eu
ton.
When Bob worked wi
h free improvising
musicians, Abana f
or instance, he wo
uld use a text but
the musicians woul
d not, or, if they
were given one by
Bob, they would no
t use it.
This was also true
Of Oral Complex: B

ey texts generated by a
heat process akin to ear
ly fax machines, but Ste
ve, who had developed th
e text with me, he was t
he computer programmer,
took no notice of the te
xt in performance. These
early computer printouts
had the same air or immi
d iacy that mimeographed
text had unlike today's
ink jet and laser printe
rs.

ed maybe d
ically dif
tly by differing sets of performers in differing
times and places.
When to stop? A question that could only be asked
with the eyes or sensed with the ears; but was not
always asked, mostly not, as stopping always happe
ned appropriately or not: always the text realised.

was a skill as well as
an art that could be a
bsorbed, unconsciously

(leave the last paragraph in)

learnt, the piece in i
mprovised performance
guiding its own realis
ation, and the same pi
ece r
ealis
ramat
feren
in differeing

ob and I would use
a text to improvise
from but John Whiti
ng, so
nd and
electr
onics,
had a
text,

as far as I remembe
r, but, because of
the technical compl
exity, we would hav
e a run-through ses
sion and John would
work out how he wan
ed to manipulate an
augment our voices
in real time perfor
mance and quadrapho
nic sound space. We
had to listen inte
tly at the piece de

veloping by us a
nds at the same t
ime without us.

maroon mud.

Lower Green Farm

Ken Edwards

Lower Green Farm was not a farm at all but an Italianate six-bedroom, two-storey house set in a rambling garden off an unmade road, in the outer London suburbs of Orpington, Kent. It was right in the path of the proposed route of the M25, London's new orbital route, and had therefore been condemned and vacated. This was August 1977. I was given the option to live there temporarily by Patchwork, a West London-based housing association specialising in refurbishing empty homes on a self-help basis for people who wanted to live communally – a form of licensed squatting, in effect.

For the previous two to three years I had been involved with Patchwork in London while alternating periods of unemployment with teaching English to foreign business students and working as part-time administrator for a small educational charity in Bayswater. And trying to write poetry inspired by Lorca, Ginsberg, Olson, Raworth, Harwood, Roy Fisher, and short fiction inspired by Kafka and Beckett, and running off pamphlets, inspired by the small press explosion, on a combination of a heavy manual typewriter and an unreliable Roneo duplicator (mimeograph machine): poetry by Mike Dobbie (very energetic and active at the time but disappeared from the poetry scene soon after), Paul Brown (more or less ditto ten years later), Tina Fulker (who died young), Paul Matthews, Robert Hampson, Peter Barry, myself, under the imprint Share Publications.

In 1975, my love for US poetry and music had prompted me to set off to see America for myself. I was skint, but my sister worked for British Airways, so I was able to fly to New York for a 10% fare. And a Greyhound Bus pass for three weeks was relatively cheap, so I took off from there for the West Coast, unaware just how vast the country was. Three days travelling coast to coast, reading Paul Blackburn and Lorca's New York poems by day and sleeping on the bus through the night because I had no money for hotels. In San Francisco, a poet I barely knew, Geoffrey Cook, who had translated Catullus, offered me the floor of his apartment for a couple of nights. And then back all the way to New York, where Rhoda Bodzin, the woman who had found me a place to kip, invited me to dinner at her boyfriend's West Side apartment. His name was Richard Fitz, a contemporary classical percussionist. The other guests were James Sherry and his then wife. We only discovered towards the end of the evening that we were both interested in the same kinds of poetry. He was about to start *Roof* magazine.

Back in London, I began a correspondence with him which also led to contact with Charles Bernstein and Bruce Andrews, who were embarking on *L=A=N=G=U=A=G=E*.

There were poetry readings in the upper rooms of London pubs such as the Enterprise in Camden Town, hosted by Paul Brown and by the Dadaist Bernard Kelly. Sound poetry happened, usually under the auspices of Bob Cobbing, ever the gruff but kindly uncle, and involving the likes of Bill Griffiths and Paula Claire. I rarely went to Bob's Writers Forum workshops, where there was an "anything goes" ethos, with no overt critical analysis but where, as Robert Sheppard reminded me much later, a grunt of approval from Bob after you had read your poem was much prized.

Nine months went by, and the eccentric director of the educational charity I'd been working at part-time called me in. He had a problem concerning a child: 13-year-old Heather McCartney, daughter of Linda and step-daughter of Paul. The McCartneys were going on a tour of the USA with Wings and wanted to take their children with them, but the head-teacher of Heather's school (a friend of his) had ruled she couldn't absent herself during term time unless they took a private tutor. I had a PGCE, although I had never in the event taken up a school teaching job. Was I free? Could I do the gig?

And so in May 1976 I was back in the States for two months. This time my flight was paid for and instead of sleeping on people's floors I found myself in a suite at the St Regis Sheraton in New York. Instead of the Greyhound bus, I was flown to Chicago, and subsequently to Los Angeles (the Holiday Inn, Hollywood), following the McCartney family, occasionally giving Heather a lesson in Maths and English, occasionally attending a Wings gig. This is a whole other story, and there is not the space for it here. I renewed my acquaintance with my US poet friends under very different circumstances.

Back again to London in the hot summer of 1976. Unsettled, restless. No job. The shared Patchwork household in Bayswater that I'd been part of was breaking up. I had a chance to return as sole tenant to the flat off Westbourne Grove I'd shared as a student five years previously, and I appreciated the newly found personal space. The Roneo mimeograph machine went with me. I wrote poetry, corresponded with other poets, churned out pamphlets, signed on or did casual work. My 1978 Galloping Dog Press book, *Drumming & Poems*, the best thing I had written yet, comes from this period. I had short stories published in a prestigious Arts Council anthology, in *Transatlantic Review* and in Emma Tennant's literary newspaper *Bananas*. At a party at Emma Tennant's London house attended by Harold Pinter and Lady Antonia Fraser I met and talked for an hour with an inebriated and jovial J. G. Ballard, one of my heroes. I was groomed for literary stardom by an editor at a major publishing house who admired my experimental short fiction and "wanted to see a novel", but I couldn't produce one.

A year went by. One day, the following summer, the gas was cut off because the landlady hadn't paid the bill. And then suddenly she informed me she was selling up, and I was threatened with eviction. That was when I heard Patchwork had been offered the use of Lower Green Farm, Orpington, by Bromley Borough Council for up to two years. I was told it was mine if I could put together a group to live there and maintain the property until eventual demolition.

Undeterred by previous disappointments in shared living, I'd been nurturing idealistic dreams of a community of poets, artists and musicians. So I went down to Orpington to have a look at the property, along with Robert Hampson, whom I was helping to edit the sixth issue of *Alembic* magazine (which included James Sherry, among other American poets). It was a warm day, with storms threatening the Greater London area. Elvis Presley's death had just been announced on the radio. The abandoned house had wood-panelling in the large downstairs rooms and a columned portico in front, and the garden was impenetrably overgrown. It seemed a long way from the centre of things. But it was a haven. It was beautiful.

Little more than a month later, we were in, Robert with a houseful of furniture he'd been offered for free in exchange for helping with the house clearance. David Miller, to whom *Alembic* 6 had been dedicated (he lived near me in Notting Hill), had been interested in joining us, but eventually declined; an Australian friend of his, Norman, was the first to move in but had been spooked by the isolation and escaped back to London. We interviewed prospective residents, and among the first applicants were Erik Vonna-Michell, a Norwegian-American artist of a somewhat neo-Dada persuasion, and his German wife Muthis. They had been living in Berlin for some years. We all took to each other. We had English poet friends in common: Allen Fisher (Erik worked at the War on Want print shop with Allen's Aloes Books associate, Jim Pennington), cris cheek, Lawrence Upton, Ulli Freer.

Erik, a big man with piercing blue eyes and a huge black beard (he once told me he had never shaved in his life), turned out to be a major presence at Lower Green Farm. His role on the seventh, 'Assemblage' issue of *Alembic*, the first to be produced at Lower Green Farm, included block-printing every wraparound cover individually – no two covers of this issue are quite the same – and also providing the most bizarre of all the contributions. In January 1978, Robert and I had sent a letter of invitation to 60 poets and artists asking them to contribute 200 copies of up to four A4 pages of material, which we proposed to collate without further editing to form the issue. Erik's contribution was two sheets of sandpaper of different grades sandwiching a blank sheet of paper. He explained that the gradual erosion of this middle sheet constituted the content of the artwork.

Most other residents of the house didn't stay long nor did they participate in the artistic activities. A young Glaswegian called Sandy whose sole interests seemed to be beer and weed, a former girlfriend of mine called Marie, and another young woman, a ballet student called Nicolette, all came and went. A friend of Nicolette's asked Erik why he'd enjoyed living in Berlin, as she was thinking of going there, and he replied. "Because it's full of crazy people doing meaningless things."

Two who stayed a bit longer were Steve and Tomo, a couple who were mime artists. He was English, she Japanese. He spoke no Japanese at all, and her English was rudimentary; but they seemed inordinately fond of each other, and communicated mainly in mime. They had been promised employment as extras in chimpanzee costumes on a new film version of *Tarzan*, but filming was delayed and they never got the call. So they went to Japan instead. (Many years later, I happened to be wandering among the crowds round the Pompidou Centre in Paris, and there they were surrounded by fascinated spectators, doing their chilled-out chimpanzee act, in everyday clothes – they were astonishing.)

I was being hassled at the Orpington benefit office, so I had to find employment but there was none locally. I was offered a part-time admin job for a small voluntary organisation working with homelessness projects in Camberwell, South London; and so I started commuting, cycling from Lower Green Farm to Orpington rail station, travelling with the bike by train to Brixton, cycling from there to Camberwell Road. It was not ideal, but the people and the work they doing were interesting and the pay was good. I acquired my first-ever credit card.

In summer 1978, Robert, Erik and I organised three "Saturday courses" at Lower Green Farm. On three successive Saturdays about a dozen people, including Maggie O'Sullivan, whom I met for the first time, travelled from London to spend the day at the house (with lunch cooked by Erik) listening to presentations about poetry. First on was Allen Fisher, who spoke about his use of music by Bach, Beethoven and Stockhausen as structural grids for his poetry, and more generally about pattern-making and procedure in process-driven art work. Bob Cobbing, when his turn came, spent the entire Saturday doing poetry and sound rather than talking about it – he was never a theorist. The only theoretical pronouncement I ever heard him make was that every effort should be taken to make your poem "more like it is". Which actually is quite as profound as it is enigmatic. (The British Library has a recording of his contribution.)

The third protagonist in this series was Eric Mottram. He was very important to me as a teacher and mentor, as he was to countless people. The first ever Reader in American Studies at London University, he had been my tutor for a year when I was an undergraduate at King's College in the late 1960s/early 70s, later becoming a friend; and it is safe to say my life might have taken a very different course had I not come under his influence. His surviving writings, including his poetry, in my opinion do not adequately reflect his brilliance as a teacher. The text of his Orpington talk survives as a cassette.

A suite of poems I wrote in Lower Green Farm became the book *Tilth*, published by Galloping Dog Press with the house pictured in a wraparound cover, screen-printed by Erik Vonna-Michell.

One further issue of *Alembic*, No 8, edited by me and printed by Erik, who was now employed as Patchwork's printer, was produced at

Lower Green Farm. It included poetry by Eric Mottram and by two more Americans Robert and I had been in contact with: Lyn Hejinian and Rae Armantrout. Even as it appeared, I was already becoming frustrated by the slow and complex business of producing a poetry magazine. Inspired by the example of $L=A=N=G=U=A=G=E$, and its vigorous exchange of views, I conceived a monthly poetry newsletter including poems, essays on poetics and news about poetry, each issue of which would be mimeographed, collated and instantly posted off to anyone interested. Actually, a blog or a webzine before there was any such thing as the internet. I ran off the first issue, ten pages, on my Roneo, and sent it to 40 people. I called it *Reality Studios*.

But my day job was taking me further from life in Orpington, and the commuting was becoming tedious. Later in the year, I was offered my own flat – a permanent tenancy – in a housing co-operative near Elephant & Castle, a short walk from my place of employment. It was an offer I could not possibly refuse, particularly as the short-life licence agreement for Lower Green Farm might be terminated at any time. And so early in 1979 I moved back to London. The others stayed on until Patchwork had to surrender the house.

When I look back on it, that period of my life, encompassing no more than four years, including eighteen months at Lower Green Farm, seems like a dream that had endless branchings. How did we survive? How did we make contact with each other? Without the instant and pervasive electronic communications of today, it seems that chance encounters must have dictated events. I have written here about poetry, but there was a hell of a lot else going on that was important to me: music (new wave rock, reggae, jazz and free improvisation), performance art, film (not just experimental independent film but ground-breaking directors such as Scorsese, Altman, Herzog, Fassbinder making box-office movies that mattered), and a sense that the life had not yet been – it was soon to be – crushed out of mainstream politics.

I continued to edit *Reality Studios* for the next ten years. Mimeograph was abandoned – I can't remember what happened to the Roneo – first in favour of photocopying, and then litho printing and perfect binding. (Recently, all 1,000 pages of the complete run were digitised by the University of Pennsylvania / *Jacket2*, with the object of making them available online.) *Alembic* 9, scheduled to be edited by Robert

Hampson, never appeared. With Allen Fisher and Paul Brown, I curated a series of poetry readings and performances under the name of RASP in a community hall attached to the housing co-operative in Elephant & Castle. In 1993, Reality Studios as an imprint was to merge with Wendy Mulford's Street Editions and become Reality Street.

Eric Mottram, Bob Cobbing, Bill Griffiths died. After several years of occasional meetings, I eventually lost contact with Erik and Muthis Vonna-Michell, but this year discovered their son Tris (born 1982), a text-based performance artist, had been shortlisted for the Turner Prize.

The M25 eventually took a different route and did not go through Lower Green Farm. But I later heard the house had been demolished in any case to make way for a new estate.

Climbing the Twisty Staircase:
"London" 1970-85

PETER BARRY

I lived in London for just eleven years in all, from 1967 to 1976, and then for the academic years 1977-8 and 1979-80. So for the purposes of this piece I am treating "London" as a moveable feast which is situated both in the mind (in the Poundian sense, as "the city now in the mind indestructible") and in the heart (in the sense embodied in Carlos Bulusan's great memoir *America is in the Heart*). From 1980 onwards I lived in Southampton for fifteen years, so London was easily accessible, and I was able to visit for poetry readings, which always seem to be above a pub in a room at the top of a twisty staircase. I was brought up above a pub, so I felt at home in those rooms – usually dim and slightly faded, with brown-marmalade panelling.[1] Amazingly, many of these upper rooms have survived – I was last in one for a 'Blue Bus' reading – and they still have that oddly-familiar mismatch between the room (its shape, size, furnishing, and so on) and what goes on it.

In a very different kind of room – a small lecture theatre equipped with up-to-the-minute electronics that no one can understand – I recently attended a paper about collaborative practices and allegiances in the avant-garde (by Claire MacDonald, who worked in community theatre collectives in Leeds in the 1970s and 80s). The speaker mentioned the implicit "passing of forms from hand to hand among men" and the "responsive hand to hand gesture" with which influences grow and become significant in groups for whom writing a manifesto or a detailed programme of poetics would have seemed pretentious, or just unnecessary. I made the connection with *CLASP*, which gestures towards the same metaphor of forms of interaction which are tacit and tactile, and nurtured by friendships and familiarities, rather than by following an agreed set of propositions and practices that are given common assent and approval.

For many years, in my recollection of them, the voices encountered in those upper rooms remained the same welcome and familiar ones. There were people I didn't see often, but when I did see them, the setting was the customary one, and we picked up the conversation we had been engaged on a couple of years previously, and took it further. But the faces got steadily older, and there was a sense that the innovative poetry movement might have reached its plateau. Then, at an Iain Sinclair conference at Greenwich University about a decade ago, I noticed that a whole new generation of innovative poets had arrived, and that a new generation of academics were writing about them (in many cases, these poets and academics were the same people).[2] Also, the passing of forms was no longer just between men (Reality Street's *Out of Everywhere* anthology of innovative poetry by women advanced and consolidated this change.)[3] The gender shift has led to the criticism that the reading venues above pubs are not really gender neutral, and that, in this regard, the academic seminar room might be a more suitable place for poetry readings to take place.

But the effect of this would be to take innovative poetry out of public space and into the classroom, thereby reducing the fruitful tension between these two realms. From 1970 to 1985, one of my main preoccupations was to achieve a balance of some kind between the untidy, counter-cultural world of innovative poetry, and the academic world of tightly-constructed critical essays and chapters in which I was trying to get established. I first published a full-scale academic essay in 1976 (it was on Joyce's *Ulysses* and *The Waste Land*) and in 1977 I was slightly ashamed to have a poem in the Arts Council's anthology *New Poetry 1*, because it was edited by Charles Osborne, who was definitely the enemy. Since around 1972-3 I had been sending poems to poetry magazines I knew were OK, because they were listed in Peter Finch's journal *Second Aeon*. I kept a record of what I had sent out (and with what result – if any) in a Woolworth's exercise book that I had cut in half, labelling one half "Poetry send-offs". But I knew I could not make a living from poetry, or be fully occupied by writing it, and the sawn-off other half of the exercise book was labelled "Critical send-offs" and was used to list articles sent to academic journals. That sawn-in-two exercise book was emblematic of an intellectual and social tension in my life, about which I worried quite a lot. At an academic interview (in about 1978) I was asked what kind of poetry I wrote, and, feeling the need to bear public witness, I said that I wrote non-academic poetry. No job offer was forthcoming, needless to say.

In the early years, I was a regular sender-off of poetry and occasionally also sent out academic essays, but as the '70s went into the '80s, the balance swung the other way, and my hit-rate became much higher with the critical essays. I also began to write academic essays about innovative poetry, but in those days in the UK, no such academic field existed. So far as I know, Eric Mottram never published anything on the topic in an established academic journal or with a university press, and I first managed to do so only in the mid-1980s with essays about poets who were somewhat ambiguously positioned across the innovative/mainstream divide, such as Basil Bunting (in 1985) and Roy Fisher (in 1986). I am not aware that any UK university press or journal published anything on innovative poetry prior to *New British Poetries: the Scope of the Possible*, edited by Robert Hampson and myself, and published by Manchester University Press in 1993.

So in the '70s, after the Alembic Poets and the *Alembic* poetry magazine (both joint enterprises with Robert Hampson and Ken Edwards) came to an end, I kept the "innovative" faith by editing poetry magazines with students. At East Sussex College of Higher Education (later absorbed into Brighton University) I co-edited *Windows* (a name we should have patented) through ten issues, across a period of four years (1977-1981), with contributions from lots of familiar "innovative" names. Each issue had a "featured" poet, whose work was prefaced by a brief essay which aimed to explain a little of the poetics behind the work. This was a slightly self-conscious way of trying to do what I felt *Poetry Review* under Eric Mottram had never attempted, which was the mediatory task of patient exposition.

My trips to London to climb the twisty staircase became infrequent, and my innovative interests, both as poet and critic, moved strongly towards concrete and visual poetries. I recall setting up an exhibition of concrete poetry in the early 1980s at LSU College in Southampton (around 1982), and then encountering American $L=A=N=G-U=A=G=E$ Poets, via Ken Edwards' *Reality Studios* magazine, and at conferences and visits set up by Peter Middleton at Southampton University – a 1989 notebook has "Barrett Watten 5.00" heavily underlined). I also recall meeting Charles Bernstein, post-conference, in Peter's kitchen, when it was packed shoulder-to-shoulder with $L=A=N=G=U=A=G=E$ people.

By then it seemed that some kind of ending was beginning. *The Scope of the Possible* was out in '93, and I moved to Aberystwyth University in 1995. In October I was at the 'Return of the Reforgotten' event at the Royal Albert Hall, when Allen Ginsberg reprised the Albert Hall "Incarnation" of 1965, and played the brilliant 'Ballad of the American Skeletons' (accompanied by Paul McCartney), as if he were just starting his career. Then, on a foul November night in Aberystwyth in 1997 I heard Ed Dorn – my long-time hero-poet, and the one I had most ardently imitated – read in the Verbals Poetry Series organised by Clive Meachen. The poet and his entourage arrived over an hour late – to Americans, it doesn't look far from London on the map, but you have to negotiate the twisty B roads to get there. The reading happened, not up a staircase, and not in a seminar room, but in a strange space known as the chapel, which was secular, breeze-blocked, and bunker-like, providing that familiar (and, to me, stimulating) disparity between setting and event. As with Ginsberg, it felt like hearing the authentic Voice of America. Meachen had studied under Ed Dorn at Essex University, and I remembered meeting Dorn's wife, Jennifer Dunbar, in the early '70s, when both of us were doing supply teaching at a secondary school in Balham, South London. Clive had introduced American Studies at Aber back in the 70s, and had invited Eric Mottram to be the external examiner, and Howell Daniels, who had taught me at King's, London and the U. S. Institute, had started his career at Aberystwyth. Everything was coming full circle. "London" seemed to be coming out of town to meet me. I had left it only in Val Warner's sense – the line is in her marvellous and neglected *Tooting Idyll* – "From where I never leave, I walk away".[4]

NOTES

[1] I have in mind here Roy Fisher's account of the various places in which he played jazz piano from the mid-1940s. These performance places included "the more-or-less disused Function Rooms of old pubs, with buffalo horns, and bedroomy wallpaper above the brown panelling". See Roy Fisher, 'License my Roving Hands' in Robert Sheppard & Peter Robinson (eds), *news for the ear: a homage to Roy Fisher* (Exeter: Stride, 2000), p.18. Since republished in

Roy Fisher's *An Easily Bewildered Child: Occasional Prose 1963-2013* (Bristol: Shearsman Books, 2014).

[2] 'City Visions', organised by Jenny Bavidge and Robert Bond at Greenwich University, 2004.

[3] Maggie O'Sullivan (ed), *Out of Everywhere: linguistically innovative poetry by women in North America & the UK* (Reality Street, 1996).

[4] Val Warner, *Tooting Idyll* (Carcanet Press, 1998).

Took Chances in London Traffic

ROBERT SHEPPARD

My critical book *When Bad Times Made for Good Poetry* (Exeter: Shearsman Books, 2011) is really a hymn of praise to the poetry scene in London from the 1970s to the mid-1990s, just before I came to Liverpool. The chapter 'Informing the Nation: The Manifesto of the Poetry Society (1976)' deals with the well-documented events at the Poetry Society (and with the poetics document mentioned in the title), which I saw at first hand only a couple of times, once to see Peter Redgrove reading in the mid-1970s, and another to drop by a poetry workshop at which Bob Cobbing read an early poem of his and one of the "Reform Group" read what I thought he'd called a "socialist" poem. (I quickly realised he'd dropped the word "national" in front of that description.) I'd met Bob Cobbing already, had visited his house in Maida Vale in November 1973 – while I was still at school – and stayed all day, learning about the politics of the poetry world (Poets Conference had met the day before) and about concrete and sound poetry. The effect of the radicalism I learnt was immediate but intermittent in its after-effects.

By the time I moved to London in the autumn of 1983 I was completing a PhD which concentrated upon the relatively critically-neglected work of Roy Fisher and Lee Harwood (the latter I'd met in London in 1974, just before I went to university in Norwich, at a reading in the Enterprise pub [organised by Paul Brown] that I recorded for my tape magazine *1983*). I was concocting a poetics of discontinuity and indeterminacy with respect to this work, but, in Norwich and Manchester where I had worked on it, I'd yet to apply that poetics to my own work, which, apart from a few false-starts, was free and lyrical, but not yet imbued with the radical pressure I suspect I could only have discovered in London.

Discover it I did. My chapter, 'The Colony at the Heart of the Empire: Bob Cobbing and the Mid-1980s London Creative Environment' outlines the readings and performances I witnessed or of which I kept evidence. It's a fulsome but not comprehensive account, particularly of the two week-day fortnightly reading series: King's College readings, organised by the scary blasting and bombardiering Eric Mottram, which included more established writers, such as Lee Harwood, Peter Riley or Iain Sinclair (though I had read there in 1981, as a visiting guest, probably at the urging of Steven Pereira, the co-editor of *Angel Exhaust* which had featured my work); and SubVoicive, organised by the non-coercive and anecdotally-gifted Gilbert Adair (one of Mottram's research students) and by the shy artist Patricia Farrell. Emerging writers tended to read here, Gavin Selerie, Maggie O'Sullivan and Adrian Clarke, for example; though Allen Fisher and Geraldine Monk read at both venues. Reading styles were performative but non-dramatic, musical rather than theatrical, a major part of the work's "publication". Sub-Voicive format was occasionally experimental: another chapter, 'Ken Edwards and *The WE Expression*', focuses on Ken's reading-presentation at which he dared to present poetics (around the first person plural and its use and mis-use, poetically and otherwise). Even at that stage I found it odd that there was little discussion of ideas among writers, although there were exceptions and extremes: Mottram intellectualised excessively; Cobbing eschewed discussion entirely in favour of performance and example. My commitment to poetics as a speculative, writerly discourse proceeded from this perceived lack.

Weekend events included the Cobbing-inspired New River Project, held in the cavernous interior of the London Musicians Collective, which allowed for every kind of performance from single-voiced readings, to multi-voiced and instrumentalist pieces. My 'Colony' article exhaustively catalogues the artists and events, from the themed 'Spring Festival of the Alphabet' (Cobbing's seminal *ABC in Sound* received its annual revival) to packed programmes of various inter-art experiences. The Association of Little Presses book-fairs were also Saturday events, with readings and displays of many of the small presses which were operated by poets themselves (Paul Brown's Actual Size or Cobbing's own Writers Forum, for example). All these events, as my accounts tell in some detail, were chances for poets, publishers and reviewers (often one person was all three) to meet. Nobody had invented the term networking – and there were very few courses in Creative Writing to teach such skills to student writers. Which was just as well: it's unlikely that the radical forms of artifice being nurtured in London would have been taught much in higher education. The whole relation of this poetry to the academy is a fraught one. Mottram's readings seemed semi-detached from any actual teaching or research at King's. My own PhD was unusual, as was my possession of an MA in Creative Writing, I realised, comparing myself to my peers, who were learned and well-read, but often only academic in other spheres. We made our own networks.

Perhaps that brings me to the implications of my title 'The Colony at the Heart of the Empire'. The "British Poetry Revival" (I was using the term in my critical work) or "linguistically innovative poetry" (Adair had yet to offer that term in 1988) was an active, self-supporting world of creative artists, pushing ahead often with no regard to mainstream poetry (few cared to lampoon "Britpo" as I had in my Wayne Pratt spoofs). Readings were often attended by a small number of people (a dozen at best out of a city of millions!) but it was a knowing attentive audience. My teaching colleague Rob Brown was astonished at the level of concentration he observed at the White Swan during a Sub-Voicive reading. On the other hand, there were very few women on the scene (I married one, Patricia from Sub-Voicive!). It was more like a colony than a capital. Presses and readings seemed unable to access London Arts money, whereas in the provinces (notably in the North East and South East) there was local funding. Pamphlets and magazines circulated within London (via readings) but seldom reached beyond. Poets from outside London were often neglected for readings and events (a by-product of the paucity of funding, of course, after the death of the National and London Poetry Secretariats, which supported readings until the early 1980s). Excited by itself, there was a psychic M25 even then encircling the city.

I am a diarist, which is why I possess a generally accurate but intermittently detailed account of this time. What surprises me about my early London days (I was busy with my post-graduate teaching certificate) was how long it took me to access what was going on. Through Tony Baker – I'd published in his *Figs* and we'd friends in common – I met John Welch and David Miller, and these kind people introduced me to others. It must have been through John that I ended up at Anthony Howell's 40th birthday party, at which the host danced extraordinarily, and it was David who recommended my work to Rupert Loydell's Stride Publications in Exeter. I met Adrian Clarke, co-editor of *Angel Exhaust* and, with me, of the 1991 "London" anthology *Floating Capital*, at a reading at Islington Town Hall, organised by Geoffrey Adkins, at which Frances Presley (another poet I'd known before in Norwich) read too. But the central London crowd around the reading series seemed a little sniffier if not distinctly frosty. The offer of a reading one week could be forgotten the next; I shared this sense of alienation with the one writer of my own age that I met at this time, John Muckle, who, as general editor of the 1988 anthology *The New British Poetry 1968-1988*, would do so much to publicise innovative writing, established and less so. I needed to demonstrate that I could write work to the general consensual liking (I would never have admitted it thus at the time), and this I did at my two Sub-Voicive readings in 1985. (They were single-author affairs, so one had to prepare two sets of about 30 minutes, the entire output of a fledgling author!) Witnessing a lot of varied work probably had an unconscious effect on me, but seeing Allen Fisher read the first *Gravity* poems in 1983 at King's, *consciously* brought a new (and politicised) dimension to my theories of indeterminacy and discontinuity, the development of an accelerated form of collage (I'd call it "creative linkage" a decade later): cutting across syntax, but preserving the forward-thrust of syntactic articulation, and the energy, but not necessarily the coherent content, of narrative. It seemed a form of disruption and interruption rather than an atomising fragmentation of forms. (In that sense it was the antithesis of Fisher's first long project *Place* and excitingly new.) My literary-critical concepts developed into the poetics that permitted my "coherent deformations" of earlier pieces of writing, 'The Hungry Years'. They are dated 6-12th August 1985, and I read them, and similar later pieces, at that second reading in December 1985. They are also described as 'Unwritings 1985-1978' as though in London I was playing catch up with my cut-ups.

Kaleidoscope of Spirits

Gavin Selerie

A striking feature of London culture in the 1970s and 1980s was
the interconnection of scenes, both within the poetry world and
across different art forms.[1] Despite barriers or rifts, there was fluidity
of attention. This is evident from the coverage provided by listings
magazine *City Limits*, for which Ken Edwards and I reviewed poetry in
the 1980s.[2] Many contributors had been involved with underground
or feminist magazines at an earlier point, and there was a general
receptivity to forms of artistic experiment. Although topics tended to
be grouped separately, there was a sense that they were not atomised
units. I thought of this recently when recalling Glenda George's
performance at the Cockpit Theatre (Angels of Fire Festival, November
1983) with an audience seated in the round.[3] At the time I described
Glenda "treading ... a half-imaginary tightrope (ribbon or string placed
on the floor between two chairs)".[4] She says that she "wrote out some
phrases as prompts and challenged [her]self to improvise around [them]
while trying to keep [her] balance." This was a kind of metaphor for the
"tentative, hazardous journey through to the end of a piece of writing".[5]
That event, preceded by a sound workshop, also featured Ken Edwards,
Wendy Mulford, Allen Fisher and Paul A. Green (with Vincent Crane
on keyboards). I remembered Crane from various performances with
Arthur Brown in the 1970s, including the second Glastonbury Festival.
If the dream of an Alternative Society had somewhat faded by 1983,
this was still a climate in which multiple things could be held in the
gaze, with sustained focus.[6]

Like other poets I was greatly influenced by the music I heard in a
variety of contexts. As a teenager I had moved freely between folk clubs,
jazz and rock venues, and classical-music halls.[7] In terms of what one
can do with a lyric, Pete Brown's contribution to Cream and his ventures
with the Battered Ornaments and Piblokto – all of which I experienced
live – offered a useful model. Here and in later collaborations with Jack
Bruce, Brown got a striking balance between fluid everyday language
and set rhythmic shapes.[8] Structurally, both Pink Floyd and free jazz
had an influence on my procedures in *Azimuth* (Binnacle Press, 1984).

There was so much happening but certain things, caught as a vibe, would transfer into poetic practice. I was impressed by vocalist Norma Winstone's ability to combine the frenzied and the gently melodic.[9] At another level David Munrow was an inspiring figure, someone who recovered the sound of ancient instruments but put them to use in novel contexts, such as the *Anthems in Eden* suite.[10] I developed a strong interest in early music. When I discovered the connexion between Dolmetsch, Pound and Yeats, this fed into appreciation of Basil Bunting's work.

My earliest attempts at poetry were songs, and in the late 1960s I tried to fuse the English renaissance lyric with folk song, bringing in some Beat sensibility, gleaned from Ginsberg and Dylan. At that time I was playing guitar every day. Another crossover involved music and drama. I saw Sam Shepard's *The Tooth of Crime* at the Open Space Theatre in 1972 and was struck by the way in which music not only featured as a literal component but also drove the structure of the play.[11] This was more radical than, say, Adrian Mitchell's *Tyger*, which nevertheless had fluid shifts between speech and song, with live accompaniment by Mike Westbrook.[12] Something of this mix carried over into events organized by Michael Horovitz, whom I met via my girlfriend, an ex-student of Frances Horovitz.[13]

Unlike some poets I see stage contexts as inclusive of or parallel to the poetic, rather than intrinsically inimical. My book on Tom McGrath – many of whose plays I saw at the ICA – contains extended discussion of this, including Olson's concept of dramatic language.[14] Beckett's practice, different in each piece, was a crucial example of voice located in physical space. A production of *Endgame* at the Young Vic (1971) stands out, expressing all the world in miniature. At the opposite extreme I saw Neil Oram's *The Warp* at the ICA (1979). I was impressed by the sheer scale of the thing, the structure of going back through previous lives, although the evocation of psychedelia lacked the ironic distance that seemed necessary by this point. Earlier that year I took part in a series of workshops with the Living Theatre at the Roundhouse.[15] These involved an enactment of *Prometheus at the Winter Palace*, adapted from one of their earlier pieces, and all-night vigil-cum-drama events outside Holloway and Pentonville prisons.

I derived particular inspiration from the work of Howard Barker, whose script for the film *Made* (1972) intrigued me,[16] and Caryl Churchill. Their use of historical anachronism, with disruptions of space and time, had relevance for the projects in which I was engaged. Plays such as *Top Girls*, *Victory* and *Bite of the Night* allow (or compel) the audience to experience different eras at once. Churchill's *Cloud 9* uses role-switch and other devices to present a situation from a number of perspectives. If reading Blake's *Four Zoas* in 1969 started me on this track, contemporary drama reinforced the impulse. My long poem *Roxy* (West House Books, 1996) draws a great deal on theatre contexts. For instance, sections 12 and 46 reflect my experience of Marlowe's *Doctor Faustus* in various productions and the controversy surrounding the discovery of the Rose Theatre foundations in 1989. I was peripherally involved in the campaign to prevent big business from obliterating or obscuring the site, and witnessed a performance of *Faustus* (first staged at the Rose) on adjacent ground.

Cinema is another medium that contributed to my notions of framework and texture. London in those days had many venues that showed avant-garde or art films. Inspired by my English teacher, who was a devotee of Bergman and Antonioni, I started going to the Academy Cinema, Oxford Street in 1966. From there I progressed to underground films at the ICA and so on. Many of these influences are discussed in my commentary on *Roxy*, 'Backstory', which has circulated privately.[17] During my decade in Ladbroke Grove, it was handy to have the Electric Cinema nearby, and there are poems in *Azimuth* that come out of that physical space and the material shown. At the ICA in 1979 I saw Stan Brakhage's *Duplicity* and *Sincerity*, works that deal playfully with layers of self, memory and thought process. His links with the poetry world made this doubly appealing.

A good example of intersecting media was a London Contemporary Dance Theatre event I saw at Sadler's Wells in which the dancers performed with live accompaniment from the Bob Downes Ensemble.[18] There were points of exchange, rather than a simple acting out to a score, and some vocal input. The pulse or timbre of flute and percussion with Arabic-like voicing, all emitted from the pit, was matched by athletic movement on stage. During the 1970s I saw a good deal of puppet and mime theatre, and became interested in the ideas of Edward Gordon

Craig, some of whose designs I saw in the Enthoven Collection (V & A). In 1982 I saw Pina Bausch's Tanztheater company perform two works at Sadler's Wells.[19] These featured repetition and simultaneous display of separate incidents. All this was grist to the mill. Events which did not involve poetry *per se* were nevertheless a stimulus for writing. It is worth pointing out that right into the 1980s experimental theatre, music and dance could command support from state bodies and the BBC or Channel 4. Poetry, especially after Rees-Mogg's *Glory of the Garden* document (1984),[20] was less fortunate, but the cultural climate retained a buzz of invention.

London is obviously a centre for visual art, and various exhibitions have impacted on my poetry. *Tantra* (Hayward, 1971) influenced the thought and layout of various poems in *Azimuth*. 'The World Backwards: Russian Futurist Books' (British Library, 1978) gave me a different sense of possibility for the deployment of text, especially with regard to word dislocation. On the whole I have resisted any direct or literal description of pictures. 'Paris 1912' in *Azimuth* was written as a counter-response when a friend tried to encourage me to enter a competition for a poem which describes a painting. The invitation prompted me to use De Chirico's work (Tate, 1982) as an element in a text which deals with a way of being. It may be partly a love or "relationship" poem but it is clearly much else. The sequence *Southam Street* (written 1985-6)[21] draws on Roger Mayne's photographs from 1956-61, shown in an exhibition at the V & A (1986), while also including direct observation and dialogue, the latter being a mix of response and overheard comment.[22]

§

My full engagement with the London poetry scene dates from 1978, when I moved back permanently to the capital. I began going to the King's College readings, organized by Eric Mottram, and in the period up to 1984 saw a mass of poets: some familiar from the London scene but also those I'd never read or met such as Ralph Hawkins. Hearing Geraldine Monk (March 1981) was a vital step in my appreciation of work that already had a certain magic on the page. The pairings were adventurous: Allen Fisher with Geoff Ward, Tom Clark and John

Welch, Sylvester Houédard and Peter Middleton, Barry MacSweeney and John Wilkinson.[23] Paul Buck and Glenda George performed a piece that involved ritual movement and gesture, as well as voiced text, over a mat laid on the floor. Another memorable event was John Porter and Bill Griffiths's voicing of the dual text edition of *Beowulf* that Bill had published – a version that avoids ponderous sound rattling. Both Mottram himself and the performers would supply background context. Reading from *Suicide Bridge* in November 1979, Iain Sinclair spoke about the energies connected with certain areas, parts of London obviously but also Cambridge. This was just after the Blunt affair had become public and he wittily traced a Cambridge consciousness back to the Templars. It was a strong reading that picked up certain threads. The 'ACE' section from 'Hand & Hyle, Ascending' was particularly dynamic.

The availability of small press publications at these readings was a key part of the scene. I had started going to Compendium in 1969, and this continued to be a vital resource. However, the King's context offered a more immediate conjunction of voice and print. At the same time, I made valuable social contacts, both at readings and via other channels. I had become friendly with (Barry) Miles, who put me in touch with a lot of people. I met Asa Benveniste at his bookstall in Camden Market and he invited me round to his house for long discussions. I got to know Ian Robinson, who provided much useful advice about writing and publishing. Other helpful figures were John Robinson (Joe Dimaggio Press), Martin Bax (*Ambit*), Jim Pennington (Aloes Books) and Richard Adams, former designer of *Oz*. On the archive front Geoffrey Soar, who built up the UCL Special Collection, was a font of knowledge and, with his wife Valerie, regularly attended readings. Most activity occurred outside the university sphere.[24] There was a flourishing little magazine scene in the capital, and this included critical discourse. *Reality Studios* (1978-88), edited by Ken Edwards, became the vital successor to *Poetry Information* (1970-80), and from 1987 Robert Sheppard's *Pages* was also crucial.

In 1981 I started going to readings at Jackson's Lane Community Centre, Highgate, which I already knew as a theatre venue. This was the first phase of Gilbert Adair and Patricia Farrell's Sub-Voicive, where I heard Paige Mitchell and Bob Cobbing, among others. By 1983 the series had found a more central venue, The White Swan, on the edge of Covent Garden. This lasted right through to 1988. Whereas Jackson's Lane was echoey, draughty and dark, The White Swan was more stately, with mirrors and oak. Sometimes we would have to wait for a group of Freemasons to vacate the room. You could see the croquet-like box where they kept their regalia. The bizarre effect was accentuated by a poor copy of a portrait of Elizabeth I that hung on the wall adjacent to the area where most of the poets performed. Initially the place seemed relatively uncrowded but the bar and doorway became increasingly yuppifed and we had to close the windows, even in summer.

The White Swan seemed to be a space where anything could happen but not in as extreme a way as at the London Musicians Collective, which I discuss below. It invited new work. There was a measure of trust between people who on the whole were like-minded, although obviously each had their own mode of operation. You could try out work-in-progress and it would be measured with a degree of tolerance. The time allotted to performers was generous. When I launched *Azimuth* in June 1984, I did two forty-minute segments. Usually the bill featured a single poet, although later it stretched to two and occasionally three. In November 1985, I read the first draft of *Roxy*, which at that time was 11 pages long. A scrawl on the draft says "written for this event". The occasion reinforced a writer's impulse to produce different things. In March 1988 I read new work from *Roxy* plus the whole of *Southam Street* and parts of *Strip Signals*.

A lot of important material was revealed or actually launched here. I heard Allen Fisher's *Unpolished Mirrors*, probably in a number of readings as he was writing the sequence. Ulli Freer aired pieces that involve movement and weirdly creative gestures. Cris cheek was another strong presence, with a dance/music element. When he read from his new book *A Present* he handed copies to the audience, a literal enactment of the title. Tom Raworth gave an extraordinarily powerful reading of *Catacoustics*, long before it was published. The programme for these years had a pretty even distribution between London writers (for example Bill Griffiths, Ken Edwards) and those based elsewhere (Alan Halsey, Barry MacSweeney). The writers were mainly British, but Americans appeared too: Lyn Hejinian, Bill Sherman, and Bobbie Louise Hawkins. Although Sub-Voicive participants were predominantly male, female poets did perform, such as Carlyle Reedy, Geraldine Monk, Maggie O'Sullivan, Elaine Randell and Frances Presley.

The next Sub-Voicive venue was The Moon, just behind Queen Square. The tiny room upstairs was intimate but rather cramped. I heard David Miller, Billy Mills, Robert Hampson and Virginia Firnberg read there. Allen Fisher did a "farewell to London" reading in January 1989. This was a retrospective, going right back to *long shout to Kernewek*. There was a marvellous moment during *Paxton's Beacon* or *Becoming* when music erupted from below to match the rhythm of the poem. Later that year I launched *Elizabethan Overhang* here. After I had spoken about clock mechanics in connexion with one of the sonnets, Bob Cobbing told me that I did not need to comment on the work – it could stand on its own. David Marriott urged me to give the line-breaks more definition, that is, in voicing the work. Such feedback could be useful.

A second crucial series emerged at the London Musicians Collective in Gloucester Avenue, Camden Town. This building was the old British Rail laundry, adjacent to the main railway track. Inside there was a large bare space with, I think, a concrete floor. As Clive Bell said, you could "flood it, light a bonfire on it, bounce rocks off it".[25] The room had a strange, slightly echoey acoustic. One could put posters up on the wall or pin things to whiteboard stands that could be used to divide or mark out space. The LMC, formed in 1976, had migrated to a venue which it shared with the London Film-makers Co-op. I used to go to events at both the Film Co-op and the Musicians Collective. The latter featured radical experiment from people like Paul Burwell, David Toop, Clive Bell and Sylvia Hallett (with her bow and bicycle wheel). Frank Chickens often appeared there, a kind of pop cabaret that translates into performance art. I had a number of friends in the free jazz world, including Sue Ferrar and Steve Beresford.

I think Bob Cobbing was the initiator of Poetry and Music events at the LMC, particularly with New River Project (an organizing force and publication imprint).[26] They put on a vast range of events including my own *Strip Signals* in two successive years. At the LMC I saw and heard Tom Leonard, Geraldine Monk reading *Long Wake*, Maggie O'Sullivan reading *A Natural History in Three Incomplete Parts*. I also heard Maggie, Bob, Geraldine and Bill Griffiths perform a text called *Rhinestone in the*

Juju. Reviewing the December 1984 NRP event, I reflected upon the venue as a space for experimental performance.[27] Bill Griffiths did a Christmas Mummers' Play; Bob Cobbing did 'Kris Kringles Kesmes Korals' and *An ABC in Sound*; Gilbert Adair performed *steakweasel*, a version of the death of Cuchulainn. There was also music from a voice-and-violin duo.

As with Angels of Fire, there was a strong female presence. Patricia Farrell helped plan and manage New River Project events. Jennifer Pike, Bob Cobbing's wife, did various movement/dance routines, and Paula Claire appeared regularly. The core group of London poets overlapped with Sub-Voicive, and I would stress the performative element that is so crucial to the London scene. The musical and movement type-things intersected with "purer" vocal activity. Poets such as Allen Fisher, Robert Sheppard, Patricia Farrell and Bill Griffiths, who moved away from the capital, retained that orientation. But the LMC was particularly suited to collaborative and mixed media work. Many ALP (Association of Little Presses) events took place there as well, for instance an evening of performance poetry in July 1981.[28] Bill Griffiths had a big role in the organization of these.

The first performance of *Strip Signals* in March 1985 featured two main voices, violin, and chorus. The more elaborate performance (July1986) coincided with the launch of the book. The jazz element was accentuated through the inclusion of Clive Bell and Stuart Jones, as well as Sue Ferrar who had featured the year before. The female voice this time was Bobbie Louise Hawkins, providing an American rather than a German slant. We had only done one rehearsal, with some performers absent, so the thing was fairly improvised. The text had to be reduced for the event, which still lasted nearly 80 minutes. That is now available on a CD set.[29] A feature not immediately apparent is that I played the bell/whirrer/siren which became Cobbing's favourite instrument. I had just acquired this from a shop in Ladbroke Grove. Bob was excited by its possibilities and soon obtained one himself.

§

The London scene encouraged two main forms of activity. At one end it spawned projects with varied textures that drew on a range of resources. Iain Sinclair's *Lud Heat* and *Suicide Bridge*, Allen Fisher's *PLACE*, and Bill Griffiths' *Cycles* have a historical sweep felt or gauged in the moment. Eric Mottram's longer works such as *A Book of Herne*, Robert Hampson's *Seaport* and my own projects were also part of that climate. At the other end there were poets with more of a playful sound programme, and their texts tended to function as smaller units. Clive Fencott and Lawrence Upton exemplify this practice. But linguistic invention was prominent in both areas, with print conditions helping to generate discovery. Cobbing, Griffiths and Fisher developed new page and book forms by experimenting with Gestetner machines and photocopiers. There may be a relationship between this situation and the production of variant texts. Griffiths would assemble books with slightly different combinations of material and Fisher's books engage with other work that leads in or out of a given project. It is a sliding, fluid notion of text, although these methods could also preserve a work's original layout. Use of simple materials, such as staples for binding, meant that material was made available quickly and cheaply.

This process was not entirely separate from more traditional technology. Someone who spanned different areas is John Sankey of Villiers Publications in Tufnell Park. There we discussed his (global) contacts, and methods of typesetting and printing. He had printed many of the City Lights books, magazines such as *Approach* and *Origin*, plus various Fulcrum and Trigram publications. He had edited *The Window* magazine, so he had an inside feel for poetry as well as the physical expertise.[30] He printed Migrant Press books and many of the Elizabeth Press ones. Some rare items in my collection were gifts from him. I was interested in how writers and editors intersected, and in the mechanics of production.

The venues which encouraged experiment were the most crucial in providing shape for my poetic development. However, it is important to stress the broad milieu in which work could be absorbed. I heard Dorn, Levertov and Rakosi, among others, at the National Poetry Centre/ Poetry Society; Logue at the ICA; McClure, Pickard and Ken Smith at Riverside Studios. In a single week in 1982 I heard Bunting read at Coracle Press in Camberwell, Keats House and Riverside Studios.[31] I heard Michael Hamburger read versions of Celan at Keats House. I went to many of the Pentameters events that Michael Horovitz organized at The Three Horseshoes in Hampstead, which had a cabaret-type atmosphere, and to his Poetry Olympics extravaganzas. Torriano Meeting House in Kentish Town was another significant venue. These were parts of a rich mix.

It is regrettable that much of the key magazine material of this period is only accessible in specialist libraries and not available in electronic form. This has to do with copyright issues and the matter of time and labour; however, it also stems from the on-the-hoof nature of activity, with modes of communication that permitted deep attention without over-concern for permanence. There is a parallel here with the transmission of poetry texts in the Renaissance, that is by oral recitation and manuscript besides print. As Arthur Marotti has observed, such poems are best viewed "within the social context that shaped them and the system through which they were ... produced [and] circulated".[32] I explore the issue of social textuality and the London scene in a poem, 'Proxy Features', in *Music's Duel*.[33] Here I should also register the importance of post-performance conversation and informal gatherings. Some of my most valuable poetry encounters were at parties given by Ken Edwards, Robert Sheppard and Patricia Farrell, and John and Amanda Welch. This is not to champion the private and exclusive but rather to acknowledge the chance way in which things develop, one door leading to another. The 1970s/80s poetry network was distinguished by a comparative absence of self-promotion. Much occurred without pressure for recognition or approval. If this was a limitation in terms of historical record, it did permit some freedom of operation.

NOTES

[1] I take 1989 as a cut-off point since around this time a number of younger poets such as Simon Smith began to make their mark and some of the core London poets had left the capital. In this case a new decade did reflect a noticeable shift.

[2] Michèle Roberts and Gillian Allnutt were, successively, the poetry editors.

[3] Titled *Poetry Pure and Applied*, this festival featured various art forms, including dance. It was funded by the Greater London Arts Association and the Greater London Council.

[4] Introduction to 'A Selection of Contemporary British Poetry', *North Dakota Quarterly* 51: 4 (Fall 1983), p. 11.

[5] email, 9.4.2014. After the improvisation Glenda read her response to the Falklands War, 'The Invincible Armada'.

[6] Within the mainstream, *Melody Maker* and *NME* provided occasional coverage of poetry. The former had a feature on my Riverside Interview series.

[7] I discuss this and other relevant matters in the interview that Andrew Duncan conducted with me: www.shearsman.com/ws-blog/category/210-gavin-selerie [five parts].

[8] Bruce for his part became a remarkable interpreter of texts by Pinter, Beckett and others, in collaboration with Carla Bley and Michael Mantler.

[9] I was particularly struck by Winstone's album *Edge of Time* (1972), but she was also featured in some of Michael Garrick's poetry and music pieces, such as *Mr Smith's Apocalypse* (1971).

[10] Shirley & Dolly Collins, *Anthems in Eden* (EMI Harvest, 1969).

[11] The Open Space Theatre was founded by Charles Marowitz and Thelma Holt in 1968 in a basement in Tottenham Court Road. It operated until 1980.

[12] New Theatre, 1971.

[13] It was through Michael Horovitz that I got to know Lol Coxhill and Jeff Nuttall.

[14] *The Riverside Interviews 6: Tom McGrath*, ed. with introduction, Gavin Selerie (Binnacle Press, 1983).

[15] The Living Theater Company was founded in New York in 1947 by Judith Malina and Julian Beck as a radical experimental theatre group.

[16] Barker has indicated that the film, based on his play *No One Was Saved*, suffered from "commercial degradation" (*Theatre Quarterly* 10: 40 [1981]), but it remains an interesting exploration of identity and a vivid record of an era.

[17] See also Sophie Mayer, 'Cinema Mon Amour: How British Poetry Fell In Love With Film' in Peter Robinson ed., *The Oxford Handbook of Contemporary British and Irish Poetry* (OUP, 2013). Contrary to Mayer's view, I would assert that feminist film theory is absorbed into *Roxy*.

[18] This was probably *Khamsin* (with choreography by Robert Cohan), staged in 1977. Bob Downes had a 5-piece ensemble, with bass, drums, percussion and his own flute/vocals. There were six dancers.

[19] *1980* and *Kontakthof.*

[20] This policy statement advocated a redistribution of resources from London to the regions but ignored the inequality that existed within the capital itself.

[21] first version published in *Kite* 1 (Winter 1986-87); full text New River Project chapbook (1991).

[22] See further my essay://glasfrynproject.org.uk/w/1362/gavin-selerie-ekphrasis-and-beyond-visual-art-in-poetry/.

[23] There is a detailed account of the Fisher reading (from *Stepping Out*) in my introduction to 'A Selection of Contemporary British Poetry', *North Dakota Quarterly* 51: 4 (Fall 1983), pp. 10-11.

[24] Eric Mottram, however, also organized readings at the Institute of United States Studies, where I heard Edward Dorn and David Henderson (separately) in 1981.

[25] 'History of the LMC', *Variant* 2: 8 (Summer 1999), p. 13. See also Sue Steward, 'Free For All' in *Time Out* (29 Feb-8 March 1980), pp. 16-17.

[26] Cobbing had been a founding member of the London Film-makers Co-op, formed in 1966.

[27] 'Mix!', in *City Limits* (18-24 Jan. 1985), p. 18.

[28] This was part of the ALP 15th Anniversary Celebrations, held at the LMC over three days. Other "straight" readings included Ken Edwards, Anthony Barnett and Richard Caddel. Annual book-fairs also took place here.

[29] *Performance-Texts* (Binnacle, 2011).

[30] *The Window* (1950-56). Contributors included Michael Hamburger, Nicholas Moore, Gael Turnbull, and Roy Fisher.

[31] At Coracle Press I asked Bunting to read 'The Well of Lycopolis', which he seldom or never read in public, and he did so, although the cassette of the reading subsequently issued omits this. Apparently the recording had to be re-done to improve sound texture.

[32] Arthur F. Marotti, *Manuscript, Print, and the English Renaissance Lyric* (Cornell University Press, 1995), p. 2.

[33] Gavin Selerie, *Music's Duel: New and Selected Poems 1972-2008* (Shearsman, 2009), pp. 300-307.

Islands & Affiliations: Sub-Voicive

GILBERT ADAIR

The first person to read, in March 1980, at Sub-Voicive – the name coined by John Gibbens for what he'd initially suggested calling something like "London Poetry, Inc.," & when I demurred we wanted something more subversive, he tapped, as I recall, a Groucho air-cigar & rasped, "Whaddabout Sub-*Voic*ive?" – was Patricia Farrell. She was followed by Roger Norman, who had also answered my ad in *Time Out* for anyone interested to participate in or help organize a series of poetry readings in the Inner Visions Café, London N8. The third & star turn was John himself. I remember not a word any of them uttered. Still, it had begun, *sub voce* so to speak – although in later years I was intermittently unhappy with the name for suggesting a one-on-one depth metaphor that seemed outmoded for all that was circulating in utterance.

At the time, I had just glimpsed the kind of poetry to which Sub-Voicive would play a host through no intention at all to seek it out. From the early '70s I was fascinated with big, ambitious novels, & engaged by 1976 in an epic novel about Ireland based on the Cuchulainn myth. I applied to do a postgraduate degree on contemporary epic novels at King's College; Eric Mottram became my thesis supervisor & dizzied me with the unheard-of texts of all kinds he would leave me every session with the need to seek out & read – all, naturally, relevant to my own ongoing novel, now in its third draft, its typeface laced ever more densely with handwritten insertions. One afternoon the talk turned to the fortnightly poetry readings Eric curated at King's, & why not attend: with no plans to be a poet, I wouldn't be given still more I'd have to work into the wretched novel. Still, Eric's *Against Tyranny* afforded a new way to experience poetry, once I decided I didn't have to have paraphrased a line before moving to the next – & found the next, its syntax likewise exploded, already if mysteriously waiting for me. Here was a remarkably exciting ability. Not long after, I heard Allen Fisher read from *Place*, introduced by Eric as "the most important poetry project of the past decade"; I felt it as extraordinary, the real itself coming through in a kind of weather-front of language. Perhaps by the time I had heard Clive Fencott render *Gulliver's Travels* in 5 minutes, & witnessed an easy cross-generational sociability among the (mostly) men at the King's readings, I was getting the sense of a community on the track of techniques "*equal to* the real." (Earlier I'd done the rounds of London bookshops looking for *Place* by Allen Fisher. "What's that?" "Well," I'd say, "it's the most important…" I had a lot to learn.)

Further introduced by Eric to the work of William Burroughs, seeking now a spatial rather than linear layout, I made a large (4 *x* 2½ feet?) collage of disparate language-blocks & took it in late '79 to the intermittent poetry readings John Gibbens was putting on at the Inner Visions Café. When it came my turn to read, from one of the cramped wooden booths that lined the café's rear alcove, I discovered I had to keep my head down to avoid losing my place. So I had no idea what else was going on. After a while I heard someone say, "I think we should stop this for a bit to talk about what's happening," & someone else, "No, I'm enjoying this, let him keep going" – which was carried by vote. I decided the Inner Visions (shortly renamed the Rainbow) Café readings should become a regular event – every other Thursday, say, not to conflict with the King's readings every other Tuesday, & not to be obliterated by London's range of weekend offerings. Gavin Selerie recently sent a partial record of early readings (my own hand-drawn & photocopied posters having been lost over a number of address & other changes) showing that through to early '82 at least we were still doing Thursdays; by 21 October that year we'd shifted to Tuesdays, & were not only alternating weekly with the King's readings but overlapping in poet selections – which had not been our (John's & my) original intention. I was influenced by free improv, which in its contemporaneous early days was declaring that anyone could break all tonal & atonal rules & produce something worth listening to, as well as by the democratic idealism infusing John's declaration that he wanted to write poems "the tea-lady cld understand." An email from Patricia Farrell notes, "There were many weird people in the Rainbow Café! – we were probably some of them." Not, perhaps, the weirdest: I still remember receiving the most strangely hesitant punch I ever have from a tall fellow who declared that only "a little Hitler" would ask him to leave for pontificating while someone else was trying to read – after which he did leave, with a backward "Hitler!" The first poet from the

King's lists I invited to the Rainbow was Pierre Joris – I remember sexy pre-Islamic love poems from North Africa & sections of *Antlers* – followed by cris cheek, who opened between the truncated rows of booths, "If I throw up five balls" – he did, & they went bouncing everywhere – audience glances darting – "you won't mind if I only catch one of them."

Somewhere within all this, John quietly withdrew as co-curator with Patricia & myself; not long after, Sub-Voicive left the Rainbow, moving to Jacksons Lane Community Centre in Highgate, & then to the first of a series of upstairs rooms in pubs, stepping into a long London dissenters' (of all kinds) tradition. Money (door & grant) went first to secure the venue, then to (modest) expenses, then to the poet. That Sub-Voicive joined King's in drawing, with some exceptions, on the same pool of mostly London-based poets – but also Geraldine Monk, Barry MacSweeney, Peter Riley, Maggie O'Sullivan (post-'88), & others – almost doubled these poets' public airings. King's always had two readers per evening, Sub-Voicive usually one, to make room for a spread of the work. We shared American visitors according to intricacies of schedules; Eric along with Ken Edwards, for example, were the conduits for Barrett Watten & Carla Harryman reading for Sub-Voicive at Highgate's Rose & Crown. As an all-round late-comer, I gathered that everywhere here were people who already knew basics they weren't inclined to rehearse; if sufficiently attracted, you garnered hints & did the homework in your own time. Not everyone was persuaded. True, the boyfriend of one of my evening-class students came with her to a reading, again by Pierre, & declared, "Everything I don't like about poetry – he doesn't do!" But true too, he never came back. Probably more representative was an Australian poet, Jenny Boult, who told me that sitting at a reading (now at the White Swan, Covent Garden) she felt generally shut out, & later ("Stop, stop reading this!") that she was appalled at the patrician "arrogance" of Oppen in 'Of Being Numerous'. Audience variability through from 1980, in short, made me impatient with the kind of rationale of what I came to call "linguistically innovative poetry" that hailed it for "subverting" the "expectations of closure", etc., of "conventional" readers. Still, "among ourselves", the most memorable readings for me from those years involved, as I felt it, radical exposure of the work. One was by a

poet who through a snarl of contingencies brought only one audience
member – making, with myself, three in the room, sitting down among
the chairs, the standard reader/audience demarcation discarded, &
the result a marvellous switcheroo of performance & conversation
that incidentally resolved my quality/quantity quandary re audience
numbers (a matter complicated, in early days, by the fact that the
larger the audiences, the less likely was Arts Council grant money).
Then Eric, reading from *Legal Poems* to a smallish audience, practising
as ever a kind of "dictation" from multiple sources – but this time
the interpellations so intimate to Central London's multi-conflicted
outside that glass seemed to dissolve in the dark windows reflecting the
yellowish-lit room. & cris, in the same room. After he'd tried a number
of things, including a song to a blurry film of railway tracks ("wrong
side of") as class boundary, never to his satisfaction, he tacked a large
sheet to a side wall, took marker in hand, had the lights turned off, &
began howling – improvising – at the wall on which he was writing –
improvising – *something else*: performing, again, the dissolving of walls
& the outside streaming in.

In 1992, Patricia having moved maybe five years earlier, I would leave
London for Singapore & Sub-Voicive in the hands of future curators.
But from the beginnings of my involvement with this "insular" poetry,
I had been struck by the lively engagement of the relevant poets with
other arts, & it may be more productive to conclude this memoir circa
mid-80s, when Sub-Voicive was beginning to consolidate affiliations
beyond King's. By 1983 I was a regular attender of Bob Cobbing's
poetry workshops; as a result, when in 1984 the 14th International
Sound Poetry Festival took place in the London Musicians Collective
(LMC), Bill Bissett & Paul Dutton read for Sub-Voicive before the main
event, & Jackson Mac Low & Anne Tardos after it (where, it should
not go unnoticed, Anne played a wonderful percussive treatment of
defrosting her fridge into a variety of receptacles). A year or so later
Bob & Jennifer Cobbing moved to Islington, & nabbed the name of a
stretch of water there to form, together with Patricia, Bill Griffiths, &
myself, the New River Project (NRP), which put on occasional all-day
events at the LMC involving readings accompanied, perhaps, by dance
or paintings laid down on the spot; artworks as well as small press books
& chapbooks were on sale throughout. In '85 or '86, Bruce Andrews &

his partner, dancer & choreographer Sally Silvers, made a rare London visit under the auspices of NRP. Sally performed at Chisenhale Dance Space with free-improv guitarist Derek Bailey, while Bruce's reading from what would become *I Don't Have Any Paper So Shut Up, or: Social Romanticism*, in the wake of Ken's 5-year promotion in *Reality Studios*, arguably confirmed the future weight of "so-called language poetry" in the sound-poetry & variously language-based intra-London groupings to which Sub-Voicive was offering a platform.

Experimental poetry and feminism?
London 1980-86

FRANCES PRESLEY

Having exhausted my research grants just as Thatcher came to power, I found myself in London with a job as a librarian and an unfinished thesis on surrealist poetry. I had to come to terms with a vast city I had never intended living in, riven by racism, sexism and economic inequality. In spite of that, after a nomadic, insecure existence in academia, I felt the need to settle down. I also needed to get back to poetry. I met my friend, poet and artist, Peterjon Skelt, who had been researching Lee Harwood with Eric Mottram, but was now immersed in the world of work.[1] I joined the Islington Poetry Workshop where I met Bruce Barnes and Johan de Wit. I went to Compendium bookshop, with its excellent collection of contemporary American poetry, and to readings at Riverside Studios, the Poetry Society, and King's College. At Lee's Poetry Society reading, Peterjon and another friend, Rob Sheppard, were there in support, while some poets I had met more recently in London were highly critical.[2] I described them as traditionalists – pre-modernist and even pre-symbolist. None of it seemed to offer a real community of writers, such as I'd had at university, or the Public House Bookshop in Brighton.

Then I went to Sub-Voicive, run by Gilbert Adair and Patricia Farrell, and knew that it was the best thing I'd found. I made brief notes about the performances, and the word "performance" itself was rather new to me, but had to be applied to poets such as Gilbert and Bob Cobbing: "Not 'reading' but performing. It does have to be a performance. I recognise that. Poetry atrophies if it moves too far from…" Then there was Paula Claire:

"Paula Claire's concrete poetry on
scattered
     my
         desk
Claire
     Paula

was her name that patterned her future work. Was that the greatest danger she had to face?"

I used a variation on this note years later in a poem for *Stone settings*.

There were readings by Paul Buck and Glenda George, influenced by contemporary French poetry. I liked Lawrence Upton's collaboration with Lilian Ward, "approximate capacities".[3] I was interested in the longer poetic form, evident in the work of poets like Ken Edwards, but didn't yet know how to engage with it. Performances also took place at the London Musicians Collective, including Gavin Selerie's *Strip Signals*, with violinist Sue Ferrar and vocalist Petra Goltz-Cofhani, as powerful as text as it was as performance.[4]

However, I struggled with the male-dominated inner circles, whether in the poetry workshop or at Sub-Voicive. I acquired a new commitment to feminism while studying for my library diploma, when I discovered that 80% of the librarians were women, while 80% of senior library managers were men. I had read Simone de Beauvoir in the '70s, but suddenly feminism became important in every aspect of my life. I wrote about a pleasurable, but also troubling experience of being dressed in a sari. It was well received at a workshop run by feminist poets, but did not satisfy my need for a new way to write.

I felt unable to make progress with my writing when I was ground down by work. I had taken on a more senior role within a community work organisation, visiting projects in deprived areas. I campaigned for the local Labour Party, and I joined a housing cooperative. I helped Bruce Barnes with the poetry workshop. I went to community arts conferences, but I was uneasy about the way in which individual artists were given grants for community work rather than art. The problem of the individual artist would not go away, and I did not accept the left's view that artists should only reflect the views of the community.

After all this political activity and community art, I was drawn back to experimental poetry. I went to a reading by Eric Mottram, which "though obscure, obviously signified, because of the tone of voice which sounded as though he was almost saying it for the first time and discovering". I couldn't even accuse him of being an aesthete uninterested in politics. I decided that I had to go back to Sub-Voicive, as it was the only place where I could learn new rhythms, new rules of form. The problem of feminism would not go away, but I had not found the equivalent of Mottram in the women's poetry scene, and supposed it was because we were still so far from the true liberation which would give us the confidence to attack, "to attack intelligently I mean". I wrote 'Highgate Cemetery', which ends at the grave of George Eliot: "the cause of Mary Ann". Eliot was something of an afterthought, but hers is the final and defining stanza. It includes the associative word play I had learnt from Sub-Voicive and de Wit, and a rewriting of lines from *Middlemarch*.

Busy with community work, politics and cooperative living, the language I heard mattered, whether it was the speech of people on the street or the false language used in news reports about the miners' strike. I wrote a poem called 'Greeks', which was a precursor of my 1990s project with Irma Irsara, *Automatic cross stitch* (The Other Press, 2000). It combines the language of fashion with the reality of the sewing industry and the oppression of women. It is also about my own sense of being defined by male patterns, whether in materials or poetry. At work I published a bibliography on *Women and the Community 1983-4*, which I was pleased to see in the window of Sisterwrite, the feminist bookshop and café. I often went to Sisterwrite, but didn't subscribe to its separatist ideology.

I saw Maggie O'Sullivan and Geraldine Monk at the New River Project, which as I wrote was "a good experience, erasing the bad". They were writers I admired, but they had also published a manifesto in *City Limits* decrying "overtly feminist" poetry as "versified propaganda" for its lack of creative risk, and expressing loyalty to the male poets they were inspired by. It had the ironic title 'Move over darlings', which was presumably added by the *City Limits* editorial team.[5] I too found most of the feminist poetry in London dull and conventional, but that did not make me wish to abandon feminism. I would also question their view that wonderful writing was the "most effective chance" for women. After all, it had been tried before.

One of the great advantages of living in London was the availability of art galleries and a huge variety of exhibitions. Women rarely featured in the major exhibitions until Judy Chicago's *Dinner Party* came to London in March 1985, with its celebration of women through history. It hadn't been possible to find an art gallery willing or able to host this large installation, so they used a warehouse in Islington. I went with a male friend who was taken aback by all the white frills and lace of Emily Dickinson's plate, and there were those who complained that the exhibition associated women with traditionally female craft skills (something Chicago had in fact deliberately reclaimed). For me it wasn't a problem as I knew my Emily Dickinson and could only think of the line: "And that white sustenance – despair", a white substance collecting in the folds of the vulva. It was a line that I deconstructed and reworked in my version of the *Dinner Party*. A few days later I returned to savour the exhibition alone, and my focus switched to the black women who were gallery attendants, and I ironically used the word "hysteria" to describe how they felt after working for eleven hours. Looking back, I realise that the first place I could combine experimentation and feminism was in the visual arts, where some women artists had clearly done both. It was also the first poem I wanted to perform, because "if you believe in those words you have to perform them". I performed it at Torriano, the reading series run by John Rety, which was more inclusive than Sub-Voicive, but also less experimental.

Then I picked up a slim volume by Denise Riley in the Virago poetry series, and felt the kind of excitement that I once felt about young (male) poets. It was *Dry Air*, which was both experimental and tackled issues of gender head on, opening with 'A note on "sex" and the reclaiming of language'.[6] Later I would hear her at Sub-Voicive. Compendium had separated its poetry section into male and female, but someone kept putting Riley's books in the male section. I could see that the change meant more women writers in the bookshop, but that the women in charge were not keen on experimental poetry. I wrote: "Why can't there be a group of women writers. I dream of it. I like all the women in the Virago series. Don't they ever come together". I then complained about one of the poets and her clichés, thus answering my own question.

In 1986 Peterjon decided to start a small press which would become North and South. I began to put together my first poetry collection. The year ended with my attempt to think of a title. I was looking at a book with the provocative, and ironic, title *Art and sexual politics: why have there been no great women artists?*[7] From there to the *Sex of Art* was inevitable.[8]

References

Judy Chicago, *Through the flower: my struggle as a woman artist* (Women's Press, 1982)

Prospect into Breath: interviews with North and South writers, edited by Peterjon Skelt (North and South, 1991).

Frances Presley, 'The grace of being common: the search for the implicit subject in the work of Denise Riley', *Southfields* 5(2), 1999, pp. 47-55. Also in *How2*, September 1999. My essay deals with the use of the personal pronoun in Riley's work.

Frances Presley, 'Hidden lines' in *Cusp: recollections of poetry in transition*, ed. Geraldine Monk, Bristol: Shearsman Books, 2012, pp. 207-214

Notes

[1] Peterjon and I were both at school in Somerset and met in 1972 at one of the first Arvon Foundation creative writing courses at Totleigh Barton Manor, Devon. We remained correspondents and friends subsequently. Peterjon went to Aberystwyth University (which also had a lively poetry scene) before undertaking his PhD at King's College, London.

[2] I first met Robert, while I was a postgraduate at the University of Sussex: I used to hear him perform in pub bands in Brighton. I got to know him well in 1978-79 at the University of East Anglia, where I was working on a PhD and he was a student on the new MA in Creative Writing. Shortly after that we both moved to north London.

[3] Lilian Ward and Lawrence Upton, *approximate capacities* (Good Elf, 1982).

[4] Gavin Selerie, *Strip Signals* (Galloping Dog, 1986).

[5] Geraldine Monk and Maggie O'Sullivan, 'Move over darlings', *City Limits* 13-19 July 1984

[6] Denise Riley, *Dry Air* (Virago, 1985).

[7] Thomas Hess and Elizabeth Baker (eds), *Art and sexual politics* (Collier, 1973).

[8] Frances Presley, *The Sex of Art* (North and South, 1987).

Inklings

John Muckle

My first inkling of London poetry was probably a reference to New London Pride Editions found in some list I was going through in search of places to send my own poetry. This would be back in the Albert Sloman Library at Essex University. It was a friendly-sounding name. I was from near London, so identified with this name, not yet knowing it was also the name of a beer, Fuller's London Pride, of which I was to quaff many pints in years to come. Can't remember if I sent any poems; if so I received no reply. Galloping Dog Press, Newcastle-upon-Tyne, was on the same list, and there I had more luck. Peter Hodgkiss, its editor, published a couple of my poems in his magazine *Not Poetry*, and later brought out my first book, *The Cresta Run*, a set of stories located in the outer suburbs of London: a small green volume which none of the capital's publishers, alternative or otherwise, were going to touch with a barge-pole. Long before *Not Poetry* came out, I received a letter from Bill Griffiths, who'd seen my poems somehow and was enthusiastic about them – perhaps for their speedway theme – enclosing a copy of his *War W/Windsor* sequence photocopied on a single folded sheet of paper. This was the beginning of a life-long friendship with Bill. Eventually we collaborated on a small book, *Bikers*, run off on Bob Cobbing's overheated photocopier.

A few years later I'd found my way through teacher training, living in an Acton tower block and working at colleges in Carshalton and Isleworth, when a call from my good friend Will Webb, who as the son of the literary editor of the *Guardian* had found it easy to get jobs in book publishing, changed my life. Will was abruptly moving on to Chatto and Windus, and wondered if I would be interested in taking over his editorial assistant's job at Marion Boyars? A small publisher based in Soho, I knew of her, mainly as half of Calder and Boyars, the firm which had brought Samuel Beckett and William Burroughs to the attention of readers in the British Isles. After a brief and breezy interview, I had my feet under a desk high above Brewer Street and was helping to proofread Robert Creeley's *Collected Prose*. This was late 1983. Marion laughed her drain-like laugh at how easily I'd tossed aside my job teaching basic literacy, numeracy and life skills to kids on a Youth Opportunities Scheme, but it was true that, even on an initial salary of £3,000 per year, I felt that I'd "made it" in London. Soon I was writing reports, and cover copy, editing manuscripts, persuading her to take on a few submissions I'd liked, and scheming away at my rise and rise as a hotshot editor.

After a couple of years working for Marion – a strong personality and a pioneer woman publisher from whom everyone who worked for her must have learned an enormous amount – I was ready to move on, and managed to snag a job as paperback editorial copywriter for Grafton Books, then part of the Collins group. I blurbed everything from Isaac Asimov and Philip K. Dick to *The Ghost of 29 Megacycles* ("Can the Dead Speak on Radio?") and *How to Banish Cellulite Forever*. The Paladin imprint had existed since the late sixties, publishing books like Hunter S. Thompson's *Fear and Loathing in Las Vegas* and Germaine Greer's *The Female Eunuch*, Jeff Nuttall's *Bomb Culture*, Roland Barthes's *Mythologies* and Raymond Williams's *The Country and the City*. Somewhat moribund since these glory days, it had been decided to revivify Paladin by launching a Paladin Fiction imprint. I contributed to this, somehow or other persuading my boss, Nick Austin, a highly experienced and knowledgeable SF editor, to let me start a small-scale Paladin Poetry list.

Our first title was John Ashbery's *Selected Poems* (1987), quite easy to acquire since Carcanet's Michael Schmidt had already submitted it to another editor, but I had to move fast to parlay this into a whole list edited by myself. I'd arrived with a couple of ideas on my mind – publishing reissues of working-class novels of the thirties, commissioning a series of "youth novels" based on current subcultures – but although neither of these were particularly sound commercial propositions, poetry was even less so. I knew John Ashbery's work fairly well – I'd written an MA dissertation on him – so it was fairly easy to persuade people that I would be the best editor for this book. I'd also been thinking about poetry anthologies for a while. One of the first I'd owned was a small Studio Vista paperback called *Beat Poets*, which contained, alongside familiar names, poems by Ed Dorn, Leroi Jones, and one by Paul Carroll, about his father, which begins:

> How sick I get
> of your ghost. And
> of looking at this tintype on my desk
> of you as a cocky kid –

I'm tempted to think this book orientated me as to what poetry was all about, and Carroll's poem, with its uncomfortable truth-telling and repudiation of a previous generation's sentimental lies about itself, had been my favourite item between its pinkish covers.

I'd tried to persuade Marion Boyars to let Eric Mottram edit an anthology (as she'd published his study of William Burroughs) but to no avail.[1] I'd also been hashing through various possibilities with friends and acquaintances on the London poetry scene, most notably Robert Sheppard. But I felt strongly that a Paladin anthology should have wider appeal than to this rather dogmatic, insular and self-righteous group, especially since its best poetry journal, Ken Edwards' *Reality Studios*, had only fifty subscribers. Certainly it would be fatal to succumb to Mottram's desire to replay the sixties and seventies, but at the same time I believed he had an important role to play in what became *The New British Poetry 1968-88* (Paladin, 1988). In the Thatcherite mood of the mid-eighties, I thought it crucial to challenge narrow ideas of Britishness, and to strengthen the hand of those who still felt feminism was important by multiplying the numbers of women included. I assembled a team of four editors to put together sections representing "Black British", "Feminist", "experimental" (or "modernist") and "younger" poets: Fred D'Aguiar, Gillian Allnutt, Eric Mottram and Ken Edwards. Never quite sure what these sections should be called, I knew what I wanted – a diverse book that brought the whole idea of an oppositional or counter-cultural poetry to the present. Now that this moment, and the resultant anthology, are almost thirty years in the past, I don't feel much like rehearsing all the various disagreements and setbacks that occurred along the way. Only to state that, as a young and fairly inexperienced editor, I kept my hands firmly on the wheel. The chosen editors had their autonomy, but weren't permitted to interfere with each other or the book's overall concept. Everybody knows that poets love a good argument, usually the same one again and again, and sure enough *The New British Poetry* provoked a great deal of cavilling "controversy", specious or otherwise; but, I believe, it did make a lasting difference to the status of the different poetries it explored.

Far happier than editing the anthology was the experience of publishing Lee Harwood's *Crossing the Frozen River* (1988) and Tom Raworth's *Tottering State* (1988). These two lovely books were the follow-ups that established Paladin Poetry as an ongoing force. Both poets were a delight to work with, and it was here that much of the fun of publishing occurred. A couple of pleasant lunches, of course, but also the opportunity of fine-tuning the elegant look of the series, working with Grafton's friendly art department (they were allowed to listen to the radio all day!) to find or commission great cover art and come up with some distinctive typography. I still feel that Harwood and Raworth were the stand-out poets of their generation.

Years passed. I came and went, went and came back over ten years ago, but I have never felt myself to be part of the London poetry scene, although I have sometimes experienced the tender clasp of its fingers around my neck. Many more names could be mentioned here, mostly of people I chatted with in the 1980s, others who were friendly or helpful along the way. Younger people have long taken up the cudgels, as they must, often with more in the way of institutional support than was available back then. Good luck to them. This honey is delicious, though it burns the throat.

NOTES

[1] Eric Mottram, *William Burroughs: The Algebra of Need* (Marion Boyars, 1977).

Selected Further Reading

ANTHOLOGIES

Gillian Allnut, Fred D'Aguiar, Ken Edwards, Eric Mottram (eds), *the new british poetry 1968-88*, London: Paladin, 1988.

Clive Bush (ed), *Worlds of New Measure: An anthology of five contemporary British Poets*, London: Talus Editions, 1997. (Thomas A. Clark, Allen Fisher, Bill Griffiths, Barry MacSweeney, Eric Mottram).

Ric Caddel & Peter Quartermain (eds), *Other: British and Irish Poetry since 1970*, Hanover, NH: Wesleyan University Press, 1999.

Adrian Clarke & Robert Sheppard (eds), *Floating Capital: new poets from London*, Elmwood, Connecticut: Poets & Poets Press, 1991.

Michael Horovitz, *Children of Albion: Poetry of the 'Underground' in Britain*, Harmondsworth: Penguin Books, 1969.

Maggie O'Sullivan (ed), *out of everywhere: linguistically innovative poetry by women in North America & the UK*, London: Reality Street, 1996.

CRITICAL AND CONTEXTUAL WORK

Peter Barry, *Contemporary British poetry and the city*, Manchester: Manchester University Press, 2000.

—— *Poetry Wars: British poetry of the 1970s and the Battle of Earls Court*, Cambridge: Salt Publishing, 2006.

Andy Brown (ed), *binary myths 2: correspondences with poet editors*, Exeter: Stride, 1999.

Clive Bush, *Out of Dissent: A study of five contemporary British Poets*, London: Talus Editions, 1997.

Wolfgang Görtschacher, *Little Magazine Profiles: The Little Magazines in Great Britain, 1939-1993*, Salzburg: University of Salzburg Press, 1993.

——, *Contemporary Views on the Little Magazine Scene*, Salzburg: Poetry Salzburg, 2000.

Robert Hampson & Peter Barry (eds), *New British poetries: The scope of the possible*, Manchester: Manchester University Press, 1993.

Robert Hewison, *Too Much: Art and Society in the Sixties 1960-75* (1986), London: Methuen, 1988.

David Kennedy & Christine Kennedy, *Women's Experimental Poetry in Britain 1970-2010: Body, Time & Locale*, Liverpool: Liverpool University Press, 2013.

Barry Miles, *In the Sixties*, London: Jonathan Cape, 2002.

—— *London Calling: A Countercultural History of London since 1945*, London: Atlantic Books, 2010.

David Miller & Richard Price, *British Poetry Magazines 1914-2000: A History and Bibliography of 'Little Magazines'*, London: The British Library/ Delaware: Oak Knoll Press, 2006.

Geraldine Monk (ed), *CUSP: recollections of poetry in transition*, Bristol: Shearsman Books, 2012.

Bart Moore-Gilbert & John Seed (eds), *Cultural Revolution? The challenge of the arts in the 1960s*, London: Routledge, 1992.

Jeff Nuttall, *Bomb Culture* (1968), London: Paladin, 1970.

Richard Parker (ed.), *News from Afar: Ezra Pound and Some Contemporary British Poetries*, Bristol: Shearsman Books, 2014.

Anthony Rudolf, *Menard Press 1969-2009*, London: Menard Press, 2010.

Robert Sheppard, *The Poetry of Saying: British Poetry and Its Discontents, 1950-2000*, Liverpool: Liverpool University Press, 2005.

—— *When Bad Times Made for Good Poetry: Episodes in the history of the poetics of innovation*, Exeter: Shearsman Books, 2011.

Peterjon Skelt (ed), *Prospect into Breath: Interviews with North and South Writers*, Twickenham/Wakefield: North and South Press, 1991.

Notes on Contributors

Gilbert Adair was born in Northern Ireland and moved to London in the 1970s to undertake research under Eric Mottram's supervision at King's College. In 1980, he co-founded the reading series Sub-Voicive with Patricia Farrell, and they curated it together for the next 12 years. In the mid-1980s, he was co-founder (with Bob Cobbing and others) of the New River Project. He left London in 1992 and subsequently lived and worked in Singapore, New York and now Kauai, the northernmost Hawaiian island. He is the author of fourteen books of poetry, the most recent of which are *xiangren* (Veer, 2007), *sable smoke* (Veer, 2010), and *Syzem: Book One* (2014), a homolinguistic translation of Blake's *Milton*; Book Two is in progress.

Peter Barry is Professor of English at Aberystwyth University. His books on poetry include *New British poetries* (co-edited with Robert Hampson, 1995), *Contemporary British Poetry and the City* (2000), *Poetry Wars* (2006), *Literature in Contexts* (2007), and *Reading Poetry* (2013). He is also the author of *Beginning Theory* (1995, 3rd edn., 2009, with translated editions in Korean, Hebrew, Ukrainian, Greek, Japanese, and Chinese); and *English in Practice* (2000 and 2nd edn., 2013). He co-edited *English* (the journal of the English Association) for twenty years, and headed the 2012-2015 Leverhulme-funded 'Devolved Voices' project on English-language poetry in Wales since 1997.

Clive Bush is Emeritus Professor of American Literature at King's College, London, and the author of some ten books including four sizable monographs on American literature and culture. The latest was published in 2010: *The Century's Midnight: dissenting European and American Intellectuals in the Era of the Second World War* (Oxford: Peter Lang, 2010). He has also written *Out of Dissent: five contemporary English poets* (London: Talus, 1997), covering the work of Thomas A. Clark, Allen Fisher, Bill Griffiths, Barry MacSweeney and Eric Mottram, which appeared together with an edited anthology of their work. He has published five books of poetry the latest of which is *Lingerings of the Large Day* (Hereford: Five Seasons Press, 2014). He has been associated with the British Poetry Revival since the mid-1960s. At the University of Warwick he helped organize the first Arts Festival which included Bob Cobbing, Roy Fisher, the painter Tom Phillips, and Carolee Schneeman's experimentalist feminist movies. With Paul Merchant, from the sixties to the eighties he organised a weekly series of poetry readings at Warwick which included not only all the then young poets of the British Poetry Revival and Basil Bunting, but also American poets including Muriel Rukeyser, Robert Creeley, Jerome Rothenberg, Jonathan Williams, and Allen Ginsberg. He pioneered American Literature and Film Studies at the University of Warwick from 1966 onwards and taught there for twenty-four years. He then taught at King's College,

London, from 1990-2006 where he was also Chair of the English Department. He has done most of his academic research at Yale University where he has been in receipt of a number of American Council of Learned Society and Beinecke Rare Book Library fellowships.

PAULA CLAIRE has performed and exhibited her poetry internationally since 1969, taking part in festivals in the US, Canada, Germany, Holland, Italy and Portugal as well as in Britain. She has published sound and visual poetry since the 1970s. Her early work included typewriter poems (*Soundsword*, Writers Forum, 1972), performance texts for improvisation (*Codesigns*, Writers Forum, 1976), and treated text (*Codestones of Venice*, Writers Forum, 1978). During the 1970s, she also took part in group performances as part of Konkrete Canticle (with Bob Cobbing and Bill Griffiths). Subsequently, she has also collaborated with musicians: the CD *The Dundee Telegrams & Other Communications 1984-86* records her collaborations with Steve Paxton and allied musicians at Texas Tech University, and *Resoundscore* (1985) records her collaborations with the musician Peter Stacey. In 1980, she founded the Archive of Sound and Visual Poetry to document work in these fields. She has produced three catalogues of her work: *Declarations: Poems 1961-1991* (with an Introduction by Eric Mottram); *Di-Vers-ity: Poems 1991-2001*; and *Going for Gold* (with an Introduction by Robert Hampson).

KEN EDWARDS is the author of a number of books, including the poetry collections *Good Science* (Roof Books, 1992), *eight + six* (Reality Street, 2003), *No Public Language: Selected Poems 1975-95* (Shearsman Books, 2006), *Bird Migration in the 21st Century* (Spectacular Diseases, 2006), *Songbook* (Shearsman Books, 2009), the novel *Futures* (Reality Street, 1998) and the prose works *Bardo* (Knives Forks & Spoons Press, 2011), *Down With Beauty* (Reality Street, 2013) and *Country Life* (Unthank, 2015). Another prose work, *A book with no name*, will be published in 2016. He has been editor/publisher of the small press Reality Street since 1993. He lives in Hastings, where he plays bass guitar and sings with The Moors, a band he co-founded with Elaine Edwards.

CLIVE FENCOTT (born 1952) began writing poetry in the mid-1960s while at art college. In 1974 he began to attend Bob Cobbing's Writers Forum workshop at the National Poetry Centre, where he developed improvised vocal performances. He performed at sound poetry festivals in the UK, US and in mainland Europe; he collaborated with Bob Cobbing and made four tours of the US with him; he also performed with Lawrence Upton and cris cheek as JGJGJGJG. During the 1970s and 1980s, he published work with Writers Forum, Bill Griffiths's Pirate Press and cris cheek's Bluff Books. In the early 1990s, he began an association with Bill Griffiths which led to two co-written performance pieces, 'The Dinosaur Park' and 'Variations on the Life of Cuthbert'. Since 1987, he has worked at Teesside University as a lecturer in digital media.

Paul A. Green grew up in London; studied at Oxford and the University of British Columbia; and has worked as a freelance writer/broadcaster, FE and supply teacher, used-book operative and as Lecturer in Media at the Royal National College for the Blind. His poetry has appeared in magazines ranging from *New Worlds* to *Poetics Journal*, while he has performed over the decades in pubs, clubs, colleges and festivals, sometimes in collaborations with the musician Vincent Crane, video-artist Jeremy Welsh or audio-fiction pioneer Lawrence Russell. Recordings have been broadcast on CBC, WFMU-FM, Pacifica and Resonance-FM and have been disseminated online by sites such as culturecourt.com which also features some of his articles and reviews. Plays performed include *The Dream Laboratory* (CBC Radio), *Ritual of the Stifling Air* (BBC), *The Voice Collection* (RTE), *The Mouthpiece* (Resonance-FM), *Terminal Poet* (New Theatre Works) and *Babalon* (Travesty Theatre), a celebration of the life of Crowleyite rocket scientist Jack Parsons. His speculative-fiction novels include *The Qliphoth* (2007) and *Beneath the Pleasure Zones – The Rupture* (2014). He now lives in Hastings.

Robert Hampson was educated at King's College, London, and the University of Toronto. He co-edited *Alembic* with Ken Edwards and Peter Barry during the 1970s. He is the author of *Seaport* (pushtika, 1995; Shearsman Books, 2008), *an explanation of colours* (Veer, 2010), and *reworked disasters* (Knives Forks & Spoons Press, 2013), and a number of pamphlets including, most recently, *sonnets 4 sophie* (pushtika press, 2014) and a collaboration with Robert Sheppard, *liverpool (hugs &) kisses* (pushtika / ship of fools, 2015). Stride published *Assembled Fugitives: Selected Poems 1973-1998*. He co-edited *New British poetries; The scope of the possible* (Manchester University Press, 1993) with Peter Barry. He has been Professor of Modern Literature at Royal Holloway, University of London, since 2000, where he teaches the Poetic Practice pathway on the MA in Creative Writing with Redell Olsen.

Anthony Howell was born in 1945 and by 1966 was a dancer with the Royal Ballet. He left to concentrate on writing and published his first volume of poems, *Inside the Castle* (London: Cresset Press) in 1969. During 1968-69, he was teaching creative writing at the American Institute for Foreign Study at the University of Grenoble campus. He subsequently returned to London and, in 1974, founded the performance company, Theatre of Mistakes. Between 1974 and 1981, the company gave performances at the Serpentine Gallery; the Hayward; The Stedelijk Museum, Amsterdam; the Musée d'Art Moderne (and elsewhere); and in various cities including Berlin, Belgrade, Rotterdam, Vancouver and New York. He and Fiona Templeton produced a book, *Elements of Performance Art* (Ting Books, 1977), based on this experience. Howell then undertook solo performances, beginning with 'The Table Moves', which he performed at the Sydney Biennale in 1982, and he wrote a second book, *The Analysis of Performance Art* (Harwood Academic Press, 1999). In 1974 he founded the conceptualist magazine *Wallpaper*; in 1993, he founded and edited the video magazine *Grey Suit: Video for Art and Literature*. Throughout this period, he also continued to write and publish poetry, including *Imruli* (Barrie & Jenkins, 1970), a free translation of pre-Islamic Arabic poetry; *Oslo: A Tantric Ode* (Calder & Boyars, 1975); *Notions of a Mirror* (Anvil Press, 1983). Anvil published his *Selected Poems* in 2000, as well as more recent volumes such as *Dancers in Daylight* (2003), *The Ogre's Wife* (2009) and *Silent Highway* (2014). *Plague Lands*, his versions of poems by the Iraqi poet Fawzi Karim, was a Poetry Book Society Recommendation in 2011.

TONY LOPEZ is best known for his book *False Memory* (The Figures, 1996; Salt Publishing, 2003; Shearsman Books, 2012), which samples and satirizes the fragmented language of commodity culture in modern Britain. His most recent collection is *Only More So* (UNO Press, 2011; Shearsman Books 2012) one of 27 books of poetry, fiction and criticism he has produced. He has received awards from the Wingate Foundation, the Society of Authors, the Arts and Humanities Research Council and Arts Council England. His poetry is featured in *Twentieth-Century British and Irish Poetry* (Oxford University Press), *The Art of the Sonnet* (Harvard University Press), *The Dark Would* (Apple Pie), *Vanishing Points* (Salt), *The Reality Street Book of Sonnets* (Reality Street), *Other: British and Irish Poetry Since 1970* (Wesleyan) and *Conductors of Chaos* (Picador). His critical writings are collected in *Meaning Performance: Essays on Poetry* (Salt, 2006), *The Poetry of W.S. Graham* (Edinburgh University Press, 1989) and *The Text Festivals: Language Art and Material Poetry* (University of Plymouth Press, 2013). He taught for many years at Plymouth University and was appointed the first Professor of Poetry there in 2000 and Emeritus Professor in 2009. He currently works by commission on public art incorporating text. http://tonylopez.org.uk

DAVID MILLER was born in Melbourne (Australia) in 1950, and has lived in London since 1972. His more recent publications include *The Waters of Marah* (Shearsman Books, 2005), *The Dorothy and Benno Stories* (Reality Street Editions, 2005), *In the Shop of Nothing: New and Selected Poems* (Harbor Mountain Press, 2007), *Black, Grey and White: A Book of Visual Sonnets* (Veer Books, 2011) and *Reassembling Still: Collected Poems* (Shearsman Books, 2014). He compiled *British Poetry Magazines 1914-2000: A History and Bibliography of 'Little Magazines'* (with Richard Price, The British Library / Oak Knoll Press, 2006) and edited *The Lariat and Other Writings* by Jaime de Angulo (Counterpoint, 2009) and *The Alchemist's Mind: a book of narrative prose by poets* (Reality Street, 2012). *Spiritual Letters (Series 1-5)* appeared from Chax Press in 2011, and a double-CD recording of David Miller reading this same work came out from LARYNX in 2012. He is also a musician and a member of the Frog Peak Music collective.

JOHN MUCKLE (born 1954) has published poetry, fiction and literary criticism. After graduating from Essex University, he worked in publishing for Marion Boyars and then Grafton Books. In the mid-1980s he initiated the latter's Paladin Poetry Series and was general editor for the anthology *The New British Poetry* (Paladin, 1988). He published a volume of short stories, *The Cresta Run* (Galloping Dog Press, 1987); a collaboration with Bill Griffiths, *Bikers* (Amra Imprint, 1990); a novella *Cyclomotors* (Festival Books, 1997); *Firewriting and Other Poems* (Shearsman Books, 2010); two novels, *London Brakes* (2010) and *My Pale Tulip* (2012) – both from Shearsman Books; and a critical work, *Little White Bull: British Fiction in the Fifties and Sixties* (Shearsman, 2014).

FRANCES PRESLEY grew up in Lincolnshire and Somerset, and lives in London. She studied literature at East Anglia and Sussex universities. She was a librarian in community development and at the Poetry Library, London. Publications include *The Sex of Art*, 1987; *Hula Hoop*, 1993; *Linocut*, 1997; *Neither the One nor the Other*, an email text and performance with Elizabeth James, 1999; *Automatic Cross Stitch* with artist Irma Irsara, 2000; *Somerset letters*, 2002; *Paravane: new and selected poems, 1996-2003*; *Myne: new and selected poems and prose, 1976-2005*; *Lines of Sight*, 2009; *Stone settings*, a collaboration with Tilla Brading, 2010; *An Alphabet for Alina* with drawings by Peterjon Skelt, 2012; and *Halse for hazel*, 2014. Her work is in various anthologies including *Infinite Difference*, 2010, and *The Ground Aslant: radical landscape poetry*, 2011. She has translated the Norwegian poets Hanne Bramness and Lars Amund Vaage. She has written essays and reviews, especially on British women poets, and also for *CUSP: recollections of poetry in transition*, 2012.

ELAINE RANDELL published *Amazing Grace Magazine* in 1968. She was married to the poet and journalist Barry MacSweeney between 1973 and 1979. In the 1980s she started the Secret Books Press. For many years she worked as a social worker; she now works in private practice as a child psychotherapist specialising in the field of adoption. Romney Marsh, which she shares with her husband, children, sheep and chickens, has been her home for many years. She has been widely published as a poet and prose writer since 1970. Her last two books were published by Shearsman Books: *Selected Poems 1970-2005* (2006) and *Faulty Mothering* (2010). A new work from the same publisher is in the pipeline, entitled *The Meaning of Things*.

WILLIAM ROWE is a poet, translator and essayist. He is Emeritus Professor of Poetics at Birkbeck College University of London and a Fellow of the British Academy. Recent books of poetry include: *The Earth Has Been Destroyed* (Veer Books, 2009), *INRI* (translation of Raúl Zurita; Marick Press, 2009), *Nation* (Klinamen, 2012; enlarged edition, Knives, Forks and Spoons, 2015), *LVB* (translation of Raúl Zurita, Veer Books, 2013), *A Cruise to the Galapagos Islands* (translation of Antonio Cisneros; Shearsman Books, 2013), *Incisions* (Iodine, 2014). His critical work includes: *Three Lyric Poets: Harwood, Torrance and*

MacSweeney (Northcote House, 2009) and *Hacia una poética radical: ensayos de hermenéutica cultural* (Mexico, Fondo de Cultura Económica, 2014). His translation of César Vallejo's *Trilce* is forthcoming as is *Selected Work*, to be published by Crater Press.

GAVIN SELERIE was born in London, where he still lives. He taught at Birkbeck, University of London for many years and edited the Riverside Interviews. His books include Azimuth (1984), *Roxy* (1996) and *Le Fanu's Ghost* (2006)— all long sequences with linked units. *Music's Duel: New and Selected Poems 1972-2008* was published by Shearsman in 2009. His work has appeared in anthologies such as *The New British Poetry* (1988), *Other: British & Irish Poetry since 1970* (1999) and *The Reality Street Book of Sonnets* (2008). Besides collaborating with writer and artist Alan Halsey, notably in the book *Days of '49* (1999), Selerie has performed and recorded with various musicians. He has written extensively about London, layering voices through history and landscape. *Hariot Double* (forthcoming) juxtaposes science and jazz through two eras, with particular focus on the capital. An extended interview is available at: www.shearsman.com/ws-blog/category/210-gavin-selerie.

ROBERT SHEPPARD was born in 1955 and educated at the University of East Anglia. He lived in London in the 1980s and 1990s, but now lives in Liverpool, where he is Professor of Poetry and Poetics at Edge Hill University. He is co-organiser of the Storm and Golden Sky reading series. His recent poetry books include *Berlin Bursts* and *A Translated Man* (both from Shearsman Books). His selected poems, *History or Sleep*, was published by Shearsman in 2015, and his 'autrebiographies', *Words Out of Time*, was published by Knives, Forks and Spoons in the same year. He co-edited (with Adrian Clarke), the anthology *Floating Capital: new poets from London* (Potes & Poets Press, 1991) and co-founded (with Scott Thurston) the *Journal of British and Irish Innovative Poetry* in 2009. As critic, he has published a number of works including *Far Language: Poetics and Linguistically Innovative Poetry, 1978-1997* (Stride, 1999), *The Poetry of Saying: British Poetry and Its Discontents, 1950-2000* (Liverpool University Press, 2005) and *When Bad Times Made for Good Poetry* (Shearsman, 2011). He has just finished a book on the meaning of poetic form. www.robertsheppard.blogspot.com.

IAIN SINCLAIR is the author of a number of books of poetry, including two important works of the 1970s, *Lud Heat* (Albion Village Press, 1975) and *Suicide Bridges* (Albion Village Press, 1979). After *White Chappell, Scarlet Tracings* (Goldmark, 1987) and *Downriver* (Paladin, 1991), which won the James Tait Black Memorial Prize and the Encore Award, he has published a succession of prose works, including: *Radon's Daughters* (Jonathan Cape, 1994); *Lights Out for the Territory* (Granta, 1997); *Rodinsky's Room* (with Rachel Lichtenstein) (Granta, 1999); *Landor's Tower* (Granta, 2001); *London Orbital* (Granta, 2002); *Dining on Stones* (Hamish Hamilton, 2004); *Hackney, That*

Rose-Red Empire (Hamish Hamilton, 2009); *Ghost Milk* (Hamish Hamilton, 2011); *American Smoke* (Hamish Hamilton, 2013); and *London Overground* (Hamish Hamilton, 2015). He also edited the poetry anthology, *Conductors of Chaos* (Picador, 1996).

VALERIE SOAR worked for many years in the Higher Degrees Office of the University of London. With her husband Geoffrey (who died in December 2014), she was a tireless supporter of radical poetry in London. More recently, she worked with Bill Griffiths on cataloguing the Eric Mottram Archive and compiled the checklist of Mottram's poems for the Archive.

LAWRENCE UPTON. Poet; graphic artist; sound artist: curator. His poetry publications include: *Three walking poems* (forthcoming from Writers Forum); *wrack* (2012); *Quarter After Press* (download through Issuu); *Memory Fictions* (Argotist Ebooks, 2012); *Unframed Pictures* (Writers Forum, 2011); *Pictures, Cartoon Strips* (Sound & Language, 2010); *a song and a film* (Veer, 2009); and *Wire sculptures* (Reality Street, 2003). He also published *Collaborations for Peter Finch* with Bob Cobbing (Writers Forum, 1997, 2012), *Word Score Utterance Choreography* (Writers Forum, 1998) also with Bob Cobbing, and *Commentaries on Bob Cobbing* (Argotist Ebooks, 2013). He curated 'Some variations on a theme of Bob' (Space) and 'Bob Cobbing and the book' (UWE) both 2011. As a sound artist, he has published a number of CDs: *Singing Marram* (for solo viola, violist Benedict Taylor), as well as *Dark Voices* and *Possibles* (forthcoming), both with Taylor. He has also produced numerous live text-sound compositions with John Levack Drever, and has had solo exhibitions of his work (1981 and 2012). He is Visiting Research Fellow in Music, Goldsmiths', University of London, and directs Writers Forum. www.lawrenceupton.org

ROBERT VAS DIAS, an Anglo-American born and now resident in London, has published eleven collections in the UK and USA, the most recent of which is *Arrivals & Departures: Prose Poems* (Shearsman Books, 2014). His poetry and criticism have appeared in over 100 magazines, journals, and anthologies in both countries. A collaborative artist's book with the British artist Julia Farrer, *Syntax of Bridges*, was launched in New York in November 2014 and London in February 2015. He has recently published papers on the prose poem and on the American poet Paul Blackburn, and in December 2014 he presented a paper at the Contemporary Innovative Poetry seminars at the University of London on the systematic-chance compositions of the American poet Jackson Mac Low. He was General Secretary of The Poetry Society in the mid-1970s. www.robertvasdias.com

STEPHEN WATTS is a poet and translator who has lived in Whitechapel since the mid-1970s. His most recent books are *Ancient Sunlight* (Enitharmon, 2014) and a selected poems in English with Italian translation, *Gramsci & Caruso*

153

(Mille Gru, 2014). Forthcoming are a book of lyric prose *Republic of Birds / Republic of Dogs* (Test Centre, 2016) and *The Language of It* (Shearsman).

JOHN WELCH was born in 1942 and has been living in Hackney since the early 1970s. In 1975 he founded The Many Press which, over the next twenty seven years published a great many pamphlets and full length collections of new poetry, as well as two magazines. His *Collected Poems* appeared from Shearsman Books in 2008 and two more collections have appeared since then from the same publisher. He has recently been working with the Iraqi poet Abdulkareem Kasid on English versions of his poems and a collection of these appeared from Shearsman in 2015, under the title *Sarabad*.

INDEX

M

www.ingramcontent.com/pod-product-compliance
Lightning Source LLC
Chambersburg PA
CBHW030550030726
47495CB00004B/1204